THE SCANDAL OF PRE-FORGIVENESS
What the Bible Teaches About Faith and Atonement

by
Richard S. Taylor

Author of

Hearing God's Voice

A Right Conception of Sin

The Scandal of Pre-forgiveness

Some Holiness Cornerstones

Understanding Ourselves: Acquiring a Christian Mind

When the Wheels Sing: How to Stay in the Ministry a Long Time and Like It

SCHMUL PUBLISHING CO.
SCHMUL'S WESLEYAN BOOK CLUB   SALEM, OHIO

DEDICATED TO RHODA

Published by Schmul Publishing Co.
PO Box 716
Salem, Ohio 44460

Printed in the United States of America

ISBN 0-88019-300-X

Contents

Foreword

DIETRICH BONHOEFFER INTRODUCED US to "cheap grace" 50 years ago. But today's popular evangelicalism, awash with sloppy agape and warm fuzzies, has carried the notion of "cheap grace" to the limits of triviality. Grace is exalted—conduct diminished, forgiveness flourishes—obedience ignored.

Influential preachers, twinkling before TV cameras, tell eager-eyed devotees of self-fulfillment that they are saved *in* their sins, not *from* their sins. Convinced that sins are forgiven, past, present, and future, the evangelical Christian looks at the "beckoning sin" as something long ago forgiven and, as Taylor says, sin goes right on producing "its shameful and grubby fruit."

In this book Richard S. Taylor assists evangelicals by helping them discover the root causes of the current moral malaise among professing Christians. He punctures the balloon of shallow thinking and shows that the very thing that makes evangelicalism so popular in some quarters is the very thing that is wrong with it. He lays the ax to the root of the tree, revealing that the problem lies in the distortion of several basic Protestant and Biblical doctrines, particularly *sola gratia, sola scriptura,* and *sola fides*.

Salvation by grace alone *(sola gratia)* is distorted because it is separated from its counterparts of discipline and judgment. God's judgment and discipline are as "set on stopping...sin as His love is set on providing forgiveness," Taylor declares.

Sola scriptura (scripture alone) is short circuited by doctrines which "sell" in the marketplace but have no real foundation in scripture. Taylor cites with special emphasis the unBiblical interpretation of *sola fides* (faith alone). Repentance and obedience as integral elements in scriptural faith are tragically missing from much evangelical teaching. One looks in vain for the believer who is "passionately anxious" to forsake the sins for which he has claimed forgiveness.

Abuse in a fourth theological arena contributes to the sagging spiritual fortune of many evangelicals. God's sovereignty and graced human free agency have been recruited to support unworthy and shallow doctrinal affirmations.

Dr. Taylor gives a timely wake-up call to all evangelicals in this carefully reasoned and penetrating work.

—*Wesley Tracy, D. Min., S.T.D.*
Editor, Herald of Holiness

Preface

A SOUND OF ALARM is being heard these days throughout the church over the deplorable moral standard exhibited too frequently by both clergy and laity. Books are being written calling the church back to practical holiness. Almost all radio preachers—who are basically sound themselves—are pleading for a new commitment to Christ. Messages can be heard almost every day reaffirming a Biblical standard of holy living.

The tragedy is that the majority of these earnest messengers at the same time persist in teaching a doctrine of atonement and salvation which is perhaps the most devastating cause of the very looseness and presumption which they deplore.

It is the teaching that our sins—if we are born again—are already, unconditionally forgiven past, present and future.

Absolutely nothing on the current scene is so enervating ng of ritual depth and moral earnestness as this. It is time the notion be exposed for what it is—a very fundamental and devastating error. Such is the purpose of this little book.

—Richard S. Taylor

Chapter One
A Moral Dilemma

I ONCE HEARD BILLY Graham tell of being stopped by a state patrolman in a southwestern state for exceeding the speed limit. He was taken back to a small town, where was a barber who doubled as a justice of the peace. Taking off his barber apron and donning his magisterial robe, he sat down at an imposing desk and asked briskly, "Name please?" Billy Graham said that he answered in as low a voice as he dared. The magistrate's curiosity was immediately piqued, as he wrote the name in his book. "Billy Graham! I don't suppose you could be related to the evangelist."

By now completely embarrassed the sheepish answer was, "I am the evangelist." Whereupon the justice of the peace stood up, extended his hand warmly, and exclaimed: "I am very pleased to meet you." Billy Graham said that he began to relax as they chatted a bit. But suddenly the justice straightened himself with dignity and said, "But we must tend to our business here. A law has been broken and you have violated the speed limit. That will be ten dollars!" Billy Graham reached for his wallet, but was interrupted by his new friend/judge who said, "But there is no law against my paying it for you!" Reaching into his own wallet, he drew out a ten dollar bill, wrote out a receipt, and gave it to Billy Graham with the words: "Now, that's taken care of! Do you have time for me to take you out to a steak dinner?"

Billy Graham told this story as an illustration of the Atonement, "Jesus Christ," he said, "by shedding His blood paid my debt."

It will help us to get at once into the possible pitfalls of the doctrine of the Atonement if we allow our imagination to build a bit on this story. Suppose Billy Graham had left the company of his gracious host/judge to immediately repeat the speed offense. Suppose, further, that when stopped again by the same officer he would have waved before him triumphantly the receipt, exclaiming, "See, it's all taken care of! My fine has been paid!"

We know, of course, that such a preposterous thing would never happen, for every fiber of Graham's being would revolt at the notion of a permanent "fix" resulting from the payment of one fine.

Yet millions of evangelicals embrace a doctrine of Atonement which is exactly that—a permanent "fix" for the sins of believers. A Campus Crusade tract, for instance, twice affirms the joy of knowing that our sins are already forgiven, "past, present, and future."

Pre-canceled Sins

Now, let us in our scenario alter the terms. Suppose the barber/justice of the peace had placed a bond guaranteeing the payment of every fine this driver might incur in the future; or, more generous yet, being as wealthy as Croesus, put down enough money to cover all the traffic fines in the world. In such a case one "trial" and one "acquittal" would suffice for all subsequent violations, on a sort of paid-in-advance basis. We would thus escape the crude notion that one lowly fine could be stretched to cover all infractions; for now, on this scheme of things, the one transaction was backed by enough capital for all fines, and the mercy extended by the generous judge was so expansive and all-inclusive that no driver—at least no driver for whom the beneficence was intended— would ever have to appear before him under threat of judgment.

Would this arrangement solve the moral problem? No, it would only compound it, for the essential outrage, the fact of providing in advance for infractions of the law, would not be altered; it would only be multiplied and hence become more patently immoral. Indeed it would be a soul-sickening cosmic scandal. One would find it difficult not to be reminded of the sale of indulgences against which Martin Luther so vehemently protested.

What concept of the Atonement is implied here? It is seen as a finished transaction, constituting a free and automatic expiation of all the sins of the elect, not only of the sins already committed but those to be committed in the future. Thus the Atonement does not make *possible the salvation of all* but actually *accomplishes* the salvation of all whom the Father has determined to save. Obviously this is what theologians call a Limited Atonement.

The upshot is that the believer who has been marked as one of the elect by the irresistible regenerating action of the Spirit is provided with an unconditional and unlimited receipt, marked "Paid in full." This the erring believer can confidently wave in the face of the devil (and his own conscience) at every instance of sinning.[1]

If our moral sense would revolt against such a gift of impunity to Billy Graham by an unknown justice of the peace, should this not alert us to be equally uneasy about a corresponding doctrine of the Atonement?

Admittedly in the case of the Atonement the personages are infinitely greater and the stakes are incredibly higher. Behind the Atonement made by Christ on the cross is the Sovereign of the universe, who has provided a means of acquittal in the gift of His Only Begotten Son. And surely there can be no comparison between the justice-of-the-peace/barber and the sinless God-Man, or between the paltry monetary fine and the shed blood of Christ. The authority of almighty God and the limitless merit of our divine High Priest are invested in that cross: sufficient surely to purchase any boon and justify the most generous flow of gifts and benefits.

Even to a prepaid pardon for sins not yet committed? "Shall not the judge of all the earth deal justly?" Abraham said to God (Genesis 18:25b). And would not this same Governor/Judge provide an atonement consistent with holiness? Which would not even appear to be a license to sin?

What must always be kept center-stage is the gravity of the problem necessitating an atonement. That problem is sin—willful violation of God's law and rejection of His rule. Such sin separates from a holy God. It stirs up God's wrath. God's wrath is as set on stopping this sin as His love is set on providing forgiveness. God's integrity would surely forbid any means of expiation which in effect would permit the continuance of the sin with impunity. Yet this is what we have in today's popular doctrine of the Atonement.

Moral Fallout

What are the fruits of such a doctrine? An inevitable tendency to wink at sin, on the ground that God in Christ has already covered it. While there are some churches resisting the lawless tide, the general state of affairs is nevertheless shocking. There is a shameful moral breakdown not only in society but in the church.

The further result is the scorn of the world. Serious-minded men and women of the world know there is something wrong with a religion that is full of moral advice but makes no non-waivable moral demands, and effects only minor, often cosmetic, lacking which can do no more than prompt bumper stickers, "Not better—only forgiven!"

Ted Mahar refers to the documentary film "Thy Kingdom Come, Thy Will be Done," made by Britisher Antony Thomas, and speaks of the "appalling" revelations of the moral bankruptcy of many of the leading evangelical stars. When Thomas asked one prominent minister if he, having been born again, would go to heaven no matter how many sins he might commit in the future, "'Praise God, I will,' the minister says with a smile." The reporter's scorn is obvious.

There is every reason to believe that this doctrine of the Atonement contributes in large measure to the prevailing moral looseness in much of the evangelical world today. The secular writer in *TIME* magazine correctly diagnosed the problem, when he wrote: "Avarice, arrogance, sleaze, fraud, carnal sin.... What more could mediastar ministers possibly be charged with? Answer: Sloppy theology."[2]

Charles Colson complains about the small impact of evangelicalism on the morals of the nation. "Religion is up," he says, "morals are down." It does not seem to occur to him that in large measure this can be traced directly to a doctrine of atonement which inevitably spawns moral carelessness. The teaching which separates security from holy living, which separates saving faith from repentance and obedience, and calls any insistence on repentance a "works religion," is culpably responsible for the severing of the moral nerve in much of contemporary Christendom.

Many attempts are made to extricate this doctrine of pre-forgiveness from these dark moral shadows and these rankly antinomian[3] implications.

Imputed Righteousness

The most venerated teaching is that of the Calvinistic doctrine of imputed righteousness. This is the belief that God not only imputes all our sins to Christ but transfers in His accounting all Christ's righteousness to us, so that God doesn't really see our sins; rather He sees us as spotlessly holy in Christ. "What is therefore credited to our account in justification," writes Anthony A. Hoekema, "is not only Christ's satisfaction for the penalty of our sins but also his perfect obedience to God's law. Because of the imputation of Christ's righteousness to us we who are justified are now looked upon by God as if we 'had been as perfectly obedient as Christ was obedient for' us."[4]

On this scheme of things there would be no ground for faulting the young man who told Laurence Wood his living with a woman out of wedlock "was all right because Christ was his righteousness!"[5] (Not incidentally, the young man was livid in his denunciation of Wesley's holiness doctrine.)

To pursue our earlier crude analogy: Billy Graham's subsequent offenses (if any) would have been denied as non-existent, because put to the account of the barber/justice-of-the-peace. *He* would have been viewed as the guilty one, and Graham would have been viewed as righteous.

Such juggling of moral realities has a powerful appeal, for it is such a convenient escape mechanism. But a deeper look soon discloses its absurdity. Here is a doctrine of the Atonement which says that Christ's death pronounces the believer as holy whether he is or not. The Bible acknowledges the peril of believers falling into sin (1 John 2:1) but the sin is blotted out in advance from the divine record. Hence there is *no sin* on the record which could possibly bar the elect from heaven.

But the sin is still real, with all its grubby and shameful fruit—a guilty conscience, inner pollution, bad example, dishonor to the Name, disrupted relations, social contamination and poison—even though by this popular atonement theory it is rendered *unreal to God.*

Some would protest: "Not unreal to God. God is grieved and will discipline; for sin breaks fellowship with God." But since the normal ultimate consequence of sin (hell) has been shunted, then the temporary break in fellowship is no more than a family tiff. The family relationship is not altered nor is the final destiny in heaven threatened. Therefore the phrase "unreal to God" is still appropriate, for the Atonement has forever and unchangeably blocked the reality of sin from God's view at the Judgment.

But moreover, the idea of broken fellowship with God cannot be harmonized with the notion of imputed righteousness. If God sees not my sin but my position in Christ, if He views me as has been put to Christ's account—"break fellowship"?

C. S. Lewis interprets this school of thought to be saying: "Faith is all that matters. Consequently, if you have faith, it doesn't matter what you do. Sin away, my lad, and have a good time and Christ will see that it makes no difference in the end." This Lewis labels "nonsense."[6] But it is to be feared that too often this is what is meant by the phrase "unconditional love," so constantly parroted these days.

"Lordship-Salvation"

There is a more worthy attempt to avoid the moral fallout of the doctrine of pre-forgiveness. It is the presumption that the mercy extended to Billy Graham would plant within him a disposition to avoid ever again committing such an infraction of the law.[7]

This is the answer of the "Lordship-salvation" advocates as represented by such thinkers as John F. MacArthur, Jr. and Anthony H. Hoekema.[8] Prepaid coverage for future sins cannot lead to antinomianism, they believe, because justification cannot occur apart from regeneration and at least the beginnings of sanctification. The spiritual life imparted in regeneration is a holy life, and is in itself a spontaneous reach for holiness; and this, together with the purifying of progressive sanctification, would rule out any disposition to see in advanced forgiveness a license to sin. A spiritually minded Christian is not looking for such a license.

As true as this is in principle, and as powerful as it undoubtedly is as an antidote to antinomianism, it does not extricate the advocates of "finished salvation" from the horns of their moral dilemma. For the doctrine is that atonement was objectively *accomplished*, in the sense that it *secured* the salvation of the elect. This, in effect, still constituted a prepaid discharge from the penalty of sins not yet committed. And while the "Lordship-salvation" proponents insist (rightly) that true salvation issues in a basically holy life, even the most ardent among them would stop short of claiming that truly born again people never again commit willful acts of sin. But they must cling to the position that those sins are already forgiven, in advance and unconditionally. Otherwise they will be forced to abandon their understanding of the Atonement as a finished transaction for the elect.

Even with them, therefore, the forgiveness of possible sins, no matter how occasional and "out of character," is not at issue, for the salvation of these persons does not depend on any particular required response to their transgressions. If they are truly born again they will have an inclination to be both sorry and ashamed. They will feel the urge to say to God, "Please forgive me"; but this would have a psychological value only. The facts governing their status with God would not be altered one whit. And if they better understood their security they would say, "I'm sorry, Lord; but it's great to know I'm already forgiven. You forgave me in advance at Calvary."

There is no escape, then, from the moral dilemma of a theory which implies that the sins of the elect are dealt with by God on a privileged basis. The one discharge covers sins past, present, and future. And thus we have a system of moral government which no self-respecting earthly government would ever dream of adopting. Special treatment of privileged persons often occurs behind the scenes, but when exposed, it is called corruption!

Only if God violated His own holiness could such a scheme in the heavenly realm be made "right" simply by divine fiat. And as infinitely valuable as is the shed blood of Christ, it can not transmute wrong into right. "If, while we seek to be justified in Christ, it becomes evident that we ourselves are sinners, does that mean that Christ promotes sin? Absolutely not! If I rebuild what I destroyed, I prove that I am a lawbreaker" (Galatians 2:10, NIV). One cannot be a lawbreaker and under the blood at the same time. That *would* be the most blatant kind of license.

No one has more security than the Christian who is "Walking in the light." And no Christian *feels* more secure if he understands the Scriptures. But it is not a security that is purchased at the expense of God's integrity.

All we need to be absolutely secure is a willing and obedient heart and a trusting faith. Every person can have this if he wants it. If he does not want it, God will not force it on him. Let us daily lift our eyes to Jesus and say, "Lord, keep me today, for I want to be kept. Thank You for the sufficiency of Your grace!"

Endnotes
1. William G. T. Shedd (1820-1894), a standard Calvinistic authority, says: "All the sins of the

believer, past, present, and future, are pardoned when he is justified. The sum-total of his sin, all of which is before the Divine eye at the instant when God pronounces him a justified person, is blotted out or covered over by one act of God. Consequently, there is no repetition in the Divine mind of the act of justification, as there is no repetition of the atoning death of Christ on which it rests" (*Dogmatic Theology* [Grand Rapids: Zondervan, n.d.; original 1888], vol. 2, p. 545. This is the position of most contemporary radio preachers and Calvinistic teachers. Recently I heard a radio preacher announce: "We are not forgiven because we confess our sins, but because Christ has already settled for them, and they are already forgiven, past, present, and future."

2. Mar. 5, 1990, p. 62.

3. *Antinomianism* is the "rejection of the moral law on the grounds that Christian grace and freedom supersede the law" (Baker's *Pocket Dictionary of Religious Terms*). Usually the telltale sign of this is the notion that to insist on the moral law is a "works religion," not consonant with pure faith and grace alone. Most evangelical teachers repudiate antinomianism *in principle* but many nevertheless teach it by *implication*.

4. *Saved by Grace* Grand Rapids, MI: William B. Eerdmans Publishing Company, 1989), p. 182. The quoted phrase is from the Heidelburg Catechism.

5. Wood's wording, in *Truly Ourselves, Truly the Spirit's* (Francis Asbury Press of Zondervan, Grand Rapids, 1989), p. 64.

6. *The Joyful Christian* (New York: Collier Books, 1977), p. 135.

7. Without doubt the real Billy Graham of revival fame would be Exhibit A of a changed nature. He would have no inclination to treat the mercy of the human judge or the mercy of God as a license to sin.

8. MacArthur is founder and president of the Master's College and Seminary at Sun Valley, California, and a national radio preacher. His affirmation of "Lordship-salvation" is in his book *The Gospel According to Jesus* (Grand Rapids, MI: Zondervan, 1988). This is a treatment of salvation which is largely Arminian in principle without surrendering the Calvinistic premises which undercut the Arminianism. The late Anthony A. Hoekema was a leading theologian in the Christian Reformed Church.

Chapter Two
Redefining the Moral Foundations

"THERE'S LITTLE DIFFERENCE IN ethical behavior between the church and the unchurched," declares George H. Gallup, Jr. He continues with the shocking charge: "There's as much pilferage and dishonesty among the churched as the unchurched."[1]

How can we account for this disgraceful state of affairs? It would be easy to say that many church people have never really been born again. The life of God is not in them and as a consequence they have no strong urge to live righteously. Undoubtedly this is at least a partial explanation. But how can we account for the fact that many who show evidence of an experience of grace nevertheless live on a sub-Christian ethical level?

A major reason is the brain washing they have been subject to by their undisciplined devotion to TV. The result has been that their sense of right and wrong has been pressed out of shape. They do not think straight about ethical issues. Subconsciously they have blended the world's standards into their Christian lives, with no apparent awareness of the utter incongruity between what they have imbibed from the world and what the Bible teaches. They lie, cheat, pilfer (as Gallup says), gossip, take advantage in business, manipulate, and trifle with sex, with loads of rationalizations and few compunctions—yet in church raise their hands and become emotionally "high" in celebration!

This disastrous development has been abetted by the dismal failure of pastors to expound Biblical ethics and insist that true Christianity demands conformity to the Biblical standard. Even when they attempt this their own efforts are undercut by their doctrine of salvation. Converts who continually hear of God's "unconditional love," who are being warned against a "works religion," who are being taught a doctrine of grace which dispenses with the absolute necessity—*for eternal salvation*—of obedience and holy living, are not likely to take their personal sins very seriously, or to be profoundly convinced that holiness is indispensable to their religious life. This effect will be doubly compounded by the doctrine we are indicting in this book—the view of the Atonement which assures believers of the pre-forgiveness of their sins.

The ethical tone among evangelicals would change overnight if pastors began drumming into their people the truth that willful disregard of Biblical standards of behavior brings upon the person all the moral and proper and holy consequences of his or her sinning: condemnation, divine wrath, guilt, pollution, and (when "it is finished"—James 1:15), spiritual death. From these consequences there is no escape unless and until the sinner, through faith springing from repentance, puts himself back under the blood. "If we confess our sins, he is faithful and just to forgive us our sins and to cleanse us from all unrighteousness" (1 John 1:9). This is a conditional promise as binding on the born again as on the sinner who claims it in seeking to be saved.

And we dare not bleed the real conditionality of the "if" as Anthony A. Hoekema does by rendering it "when we confess our sins, God is faithful and righteous to forgive,"[2] What if we do not "confess our sins"? The "if" means that our forgiveness hinges on our so confessing. No confession, no forgiveness.[3]

God's Eternal Now

At this point note must be taken of a quite different and more subtle rationale for the idea of pre-accomplished forgiveness. It is the explanation that with God there is no past or future; all is one Eternal Now. The sins which to us are yet future are already present to God, and because present no license to commit them is implied in their forgiveness. Christ's blood was shed to cover every sin, and the sins of this generation were as real and present then as now. In other words, the Atonement was the transaction between the Father and the Son which secured forgiveness as a package deal, and the sins which to us are yet future are to God as present and as covered as if already committed.

The most direct answer to this slippery logic is the reminder that God deals with us on the basis of a temporal order. Whether or not an Eternal Now in God's consciousness is true is a philosophical and theological issue which need not be debated here. It is sufficient to observe that God has created man, the earth, and the universe to function in a time system.

Creation occurred not in a flat instant but in chronological sequence. God took six "days" to put everything in place. The sun and moon were set in the heavens "for signs and seasons, and for days and years" (Genesis 1:14). Man's destiny is to exist in Time—birth, adulthood, death, and "after this the judgment" (Hebrews 9:27).

The important thing is that God relates himself to His creation solely within this temporal framework. The writer to the Hebrews says that "in time past God spoke to the fathers by the Son" (Hebrews 1:1-2). It was "when the time had fully come" that God "sent his Son" (Galatians 4:4). Neither is there any hint of an Eternal Now in Paul's address at Athens: "These times of ignorance God overlooked, but now commands all men everywhere to repent, because He has appointed a day in which He will judge the world" (Acts 17:30-31).

This time-signature of God's redemptive act in Christ is also explicit in Revelation 1:17, 18: "Do not be afraid; I am the First and the Last. I am He who lives, and was dead, and behold, I am alive forevermore." Here is a past, present, and future in Christ's own mind: He *was* dead, but He is not now. There is no eternal Now here. Christ remembers and He projects.

It is apparent that God relates Himself to the human race in adaptive and modified action coincident with respective points in human history. In God's redemptive program there is a very real past, present, and future. The variables of the past and present will determine the verities of the future.

And this is the reality on which any possible freedom and any possible morality must be predicated. Morality has to do with right and wrong, and the ability to make moral choices. Sin is wrong choice, righteousness is the proper choice. From our choices character is shaped, and this must of necessity be a process. Processes require time.

Furthermore, from our choices flow responsibility and accountability. This means that God and man can hold us responsible and therefore accountable for the way we behave. But this demands corollary terms: guilt, desert, blameworthiness, praiseworthiness.

To complete the moral grid must be the concept of consequences: action and reaction, reward and punishment, sowing and reaping. But these are temporal realities, every one. Reaction follows action. Effect follows cause. Consequence follows choice. Guilt and punishment follow sin. Rewards follow good works. Reaping follows sowing. Judgment follows life.

These sequences are not only the very stuff of life, but the bedrock assumptions of the Bible, from Genesis to Revelation. God's dealings with us consistently confirm this temporal order. Therefore God's economy of grace has Time written all over it. This fact directs God's attitude towards us at any one moment, whether of wrath or pleasure, condemnation or forgiveness. "Therefore consider the goodness and severity of God: on those who fell, severity; but toward you, goodness, if you continue in His goodness. Otherwise, you also will be cut off" (Romans 11:22).

Clearly, God acts and reacts toward us in a world of time. His response is contemporary and current. Whatever Eternal Now may be true of God's own consciousness there is not the slightest hint in the Scriptures that His bearing toward us is frozen by Calvary into an eternal salvation fixation. The sacrifice of Christ does not annul the temporal framework of morality. The conclusion must be that God's Eternal Now (if a valid concept at all), is completely irrelevant to the rightness or wrongness of a redemptive system which includes the pre-forgiveness of sins. Therefore the Moral Dilemma is still with us.

Furthermore, these rationalizations do not succeed in ceed in riddie doctrine of prepaid forgiveness of its antinomian overtones. No matter how regenerate and sanctified a believer may be, no matter how deep is his desire to live a holy life, he will at times experience powerful temptations. Does anyone really suppose that a Christian who believes that the beckoning sin is *already forgiven* will try as hard to resist it as he would if he believed he was exposing himself to sin's full eternal consequences? Theoretically, perfect love for God will counterbalance the pull of the temptation; but in some situations and times our love may not be that perfect. At such times love needs the supplement and reinforcement of old-fashioned fear—fear of God's wrath and fear of sin's ultimate potential, hell.[4]

Cauterizing the Conscience

S. Bruce Narramore is helpful in much of his discussion in *No Condemnation*. However, he muddies the waters when he claims that "guilt feelings do not come from God."[5] They may not always come from the immediate conviction of the Holy Spirit, but in many cases they do. The Holy Spirit, taught Jesus, "will convict the world of guilt in regard to sin and righteousness and judgment" (John 16:8, NIV). Does He convict the world and not Christians?

When we grieve the Spirit, which we are commanded not to do (Ephesians 4:30), we find ourselves in spiritual trouble. That trouble involves the disturbance of conscience—and should. To imply, as Narramore does, that occasions for guilt should be resolved by remembering their pre-forgiveness in Christ is to fail to face the event and achieve the truly Biblical resolution. That is found in adjustment, amendment as needed, and most of all by the sense of forgiveness which comes when we obey 1 John 1:9.

Conscience must not be silenced in the name of orthodoxy. "Jesus Christ has paid for our sins," Narramore says, "so we are free from the need to work, defend, or atone, no matter what our failures."[6] But here is "finished salvation" again, in its raw, unvarnished implications. Confession, amendment, adjustment are not intrinsically essential, for the sins are already covered.

In this direction lies the cauterizing of conscience. Paul wouldn't permit himself to rest so comfortably. He says: "I myself always strive to have a conscience without offense toward God and man" (Acts 24:16). He didn't say he managed to keep his conscience deactivated, using the Atonement as a sedative. But he put forth an effort to keep his conscience sensitive and to clear it by confession and adjustment.

Of course no one knew better than Paul that his only ultimate hope for a clear conscience was in the Blood; but not in the sense that conscience could now be bypassed. For he has just been saying that he has the hope of the resurrection, "of the just and the unjust." Now, "This being so," (i.e., to be sure of not being found among the wicked), he listened to his conscience and acted when it smote him. There is no hint anywhere in Paul's writings that he considered the voice of his conscience irrelevant to his spiritual standing.

The blunt truth is, Christians who sin volitionally *should* feel guilty. It is the only decent reaction. The guilt should continue to weigh heavily on their spirit until the matter is resolved by restitution, confession, adjustment, and certainly by divine forgiveness, humbly asked for and consciously and gratefully received. To shunt the conscience aside at such times in the name of faith is a sure recipe for a callused conscience. Certainly a callused conscience cannot be reconciled with Christian character.

It is bad enough for people in the world to have a "conscience...seared with a hot iron" (1 Timothy 4:2); how incredible that anyone would teach a doctrine which fostered such a conscience in Christians! Such persons need to heed the warning that persons who reject a pure heart and a good conscience make a shipwreck of their faith (1 Timothy 1:5, 19).

George MacDonald hones the moral issue to its razor edge in his imagined discussion:

> "I thank you, Lord, fofor fing me," says his child who does not yet love the light, "but I prefer staying in the darkness: forgive me that too."
>
> "No; that cannot be," replies the Lord of light. "The one thing that cannot be forgiven is choosing to be evil,... The thing that is past I pass, but he who goes on doing the same, annihilates my forgiveness, makes it of no effect. Shall I allow creatures to be the thing my soul hates?"

And MacDonald asks the searching question: "How can they who will not repent be forgiven, except in the sense that God does and will do all he can to make them repent?"[7]

As Christians we should examine ourselves in total honesty. Do we find within ourselves a disposition to seize avidly doctrinal loopholes for sin? That is a disposition which needs to be confessed to God as being itself sinful, and which needs to be cleansed by the baptism with the Holy Spirit.

Perhaps the teaching which has been discussed in these two chapters should be called, not just a Moral Dilemma, but a Moral Scandal. In any case, it is time we take another look at the particular doctrine of the Atonement which has created for us this painful moral confusion. It would seem that sound moral sense would suggest that a doctrine with such fallout is at least suspect.[8]

Our most direct approach will be to reexamine the nature of Biblical faith, which we will proceed to do in the next several chapters.

Endnotes

1. "Vital Signs: In a changing world, what are the indications of spiritual health?", an interview with George H. Gallup, Jr., in *Leadership* (*Christianity Today, Inc.*) Fall, 1987, vol. viii, No. 4, p. 12f.
2. *Saved By Grace*, p. 176. See also the same rendering, p. 180.
3. Commenting on this verse A. T. Robertson says: "Jesus made confession of sin necessary to forgiveness" (*Word Pictures in the New Testament*, vol. 6, p. 208).
4. It should be noted that the concept of God's Eternal Now does not alter the implication of either Universalism or Predestination. A finished transaction necessarily secures the intended benefits for the (not will be) saved. If the salvation is selective, then the Atonement is correspondingly limited. The idea of God's Eternal Now contributes nothing to the settlement of this issue.
5. *No Condemnation: Rethinking Guilt Motivation in Counseling, Preaching, and Parenting* (Grand Rapids, MI.: Zondervan Publishing House, 1984), p. 291. An advertisement in *Christianity Today* interprets the intended meaning as follows: "Dr. Narramore shows how feelings of guilt actually involve a denial of the efficacy of Christ's atonement and are a part of fallen humanity's efforts to solve its own problems apart from God." In other words, for a Christian to allow himself to feel guilty when he sins is to deny the efficacy of the Atonement! Rather, not to feel guilty is to grieve the Spirit. The guilt feelings are God's instrument for bringing the Christian back into line with His holy will.
6. Ibid., p. 296.
7. *Discovering the character of God*, comp. and ed. by Michael R. Phillips (Minneapolis: Bethany House Publishers, 1989), pp. 158, 159.
8. See Wesley's "Second Dialogue Between an Antinomian and His Friend," *Works*, vol. 10, p. 276.

Chapter Three
The Catalyst of Faith

FOR MANY YEARS MY brother and his wife manned a fire lookout station in southern Idaho. I will never forget one dramatic, exciting June day which occurred while we were visiting. During the forenoon two large electric storms, with plenty of lightning but no rain, passed over those tinder-dry forest-covered mountains. Within two hours lightning strikes ignited dozens of timber blazes, tiny and almost invisible at first, but very quickly, in some cases, spreading into serious and widespread peril.

My brother spent every moment scanning the terrain through his powerful field glasses. When he would isolate a tiny wisp of smoke he would identify its exact location and call in the report to the field headquarters in the valley below. Soon the airwaves were crackling with reports and directions, activating the fire-fighting equipment and crews, which had been ready for weeks for just such a day. Planes were soon in the air, dropping chemicals on hard-to-reach spots. In some cases parachutists were dropped to attempt single-handedly to control a blaze before it got out of hand. Heavy equipment began moving along the mountain roads, fanning out in every direction. Hundreds of fire-fighters were dispatched into action.

As I watched and listened to this real life drama I thought of the many trained firefighters who had been brought to this valley and mountain area to do nothing all summer but to fight fires. Many would say, I reflected, that they had a *negative* job. They spent their whole time *against* something. They were always on the lookout for something to put out!

But as I thought a little deeper it came to me that these crews did not have a negative occupation at all. Their opposition to fires was the product of their love for the forests. They were against fires because they were *for* the rippling brooks, the meadow flowers, the gentle does and fawns, the rolling sheep pastures, the tall pines which provided a watershed, and provided timber for homes and churches. From that standpoint they were heroes. Their lives were defined more by what they were for than what they were against.

Is there not an analogy here with what I am trying to do in the arguments advanced in this book? True, the book is bearing down hard on a teaching believed to be wrong, not only wrong but dangerously so. Perhaps these vigorous arguments can be viewed as being not just *against* something, but as being *for* something. They are for something very precious— truth, and the spiritual welfare of Christians who need to know the truth, and who are in profound danger if they do not.

Some deeply devout Christians, no doubt, will love God with all their hearts and hate sin and avoid it with all their might, regardless of what they believe about sins being already forgiven, past, present, and future.

But if such Christians are wise as well as devout they will realize that in loving God they must also love the truth; and therefore be willing to expend the mental energy in studying that they might know the truth. And it will occur to them that if this teaching is unBiblical, and if it has the potential to foster in some weak Christian a false sense of security, with the possible result of eternal loss, then arguments marshaled against it are not simply "being negative." We are not spinning our wheels in useless theological debate, but grappling in all honesty with *life and death truth issues*. If the gravity of these issues is borne in upon us we will come to see that the effort required to plow through these pages of inquiry and argument will be abundantly justified.

The Task Defined

While Christendom is divided about many matters relating to the Atonement and personal salvation, there is unity on at least three points: First, the author of our salvation is God; second, the means of our salvation is Christ Jesus and His cross; third, the condition of salvation is faith. Calvinists, Arminians, Lutherans, and whatever else there is in between which professes to be Bible-based, all agree that if salvation requires human response in any respect it is at the point of faith.

The verdict of Scripture is too clear to be debatable. Such statements as "Believe on the Lord Jesus Christ, and you will be saved" (Acts 16:31) and "Therefore, having been justified by faith, we have peace with God through our Lord Jesus Christ" (Romans 5:1), put the issue beyond argument. When, however, we begin to try to understand the nature of this faith and how it functions, we soon come not just to a parting of the ways but to bewildering diversity.

There is a very intimate connection between one's doctrine of the Atonement and one's understanding of faith. If we know what is believed about faith we can tell what must (if logical) be believed about the Atonement. The reverse is also true. If we approach our understanding of faith from the standpoint of our understanding of the Atonement, our doctrine of faith will be shaped accordingly. This will become clearer as we move further into this study.

Our only hope of certainty is to look once again into the Scriptures. We need to find there:

1. What is to be believed for salvation to be experienced (Chapters Three, Four, and Five).

2. The constituent elements of saving faith (Chapters Six and Seven).

3. How such faith is to be acquired (Chapters Eight, Nine, and Ten).

What Is To Be Believed

Respecting the substance of faith, or what is to be believed, we must begin by countering the protests of many who would exclaim, "Not *what* but *Who* is the important question"; for Christian faith (they say) is in a Person, not a creed. That Person is Christ Jesus our Lord. He is the Saviour in whom we must put our trust. So far so good. But who is this Jesus? What is there about Him which justifies believing in Him? Instantly we find the "what" brought back in the side door, right to center stage. For we must put a face to the name Jesus. We cannot believe in a vacuum, and we are not authorized to invest in the name any content we choose.

Certain terse, encapsulated answers are found ready-made for us in the Scripture, as, for instance:

> *God was manifested in the flesh,*
> *Justified in the Spirit,*
> *Seen by angels,*
> *Preached among the Gentiles,*

> *Believed on in the world,*
> *Received up in glory* (I Timothy 3:16).

The full truth about Jesus packed into these few lines can be unfolded only by a careful study of the New Testament. But certain basic implications are obvious: Christ's deity, His preexistence, His endorsement as the Son by the Spirit, the testimony of angels, the apostolic preaching of this Christ everywhere, the faith placed in Him while He was among men, and His Ascension to the Father, which implies what preceded it—the Cross and the Resurrection; and also His present intercession and His coming again, as predicted at the time of His Ascension. This was the Christ-Event, which occurred at a point in history in a tiny land called Palestine. All the lines of divine revelation and redemption converge in this Christ-Event and flow from it. This is what is to be believed.

This does not mean that before a sinner can come to Christ he must have a full intellectual understanding of all the facets and nuances of this Christ-Event. His knowledge at the moment of conversion may be very embryonic. But it must be true knowledge. He must perceive that in ways he does not understand Jesus is his Saviour and his only hope. The revelation of saving truth is always in the gospel, as found in the Scriptures, never through our own free-wheeling speculations.

Therefore, while a repentant soul's salvation does not hinge on being able to recite some particular creedal dogma, word for word, or displaying a thorough understanding of it, we must nevertheless insist that if faith in any degree is essential for forgiveness, there must be something in the mind to be believed, and that something must be truth. It cannot be fiction, or myth, or superstition.

As we comb the New Testament we are impressed with a common requisite: *a basic acknowledgment of Christ's identity*. There must be a perception that in some way He is the Son and Saviour of God. For the Jews this would specifically include grasping the truth of His Messiahship. To them Jesus said, "If you do not believe that I am *He*, you will die in your sins" (John 8:24)."[1]

As we read these lines, it would be well to ask ourselves: Do I really know who Jesus is? Am I convinced that He is the one and only Son of God, eternal in the Triune Godhead, who became the God-Man for my redemption? As I meditate in the Scriptures and pray, does such a claim have the ring of truth? And does my mind find rest in knowing that Jesus is my Saviour solely and uniquely and adequately, in a way that Buddha, Confucius, Mohammed, or even Moses, cannot now or ever be?

Endnotes

1. The undeviating focus on Jesus as the object of our faith is seen throughout the NT. Cf. such passages as Acts 4:12: Romans 10:13-14; 1 Timothy 2:5; 2 Timothy 2:10. Others will be unfolded in the chapters which follow.

Chapter Four
Faith Before and After Calvary

SALVATION BEFORE CHRIST'S ADVENT was dependent on faith in and obedience to the God of Abraham, Isaac, and Jacob, who through Moses established the covenant of the law, and provided atoning sacrifices as a means of covering infractions of the law. When we read that Moses knew God face to face, that Elijah talked with God, that Isaiah was cleansed from his iniquity, we are to accept these accounts at face value. Undoubtedly thousands of Old Testament saints were in a saved state and will mingle with the post-Calvary saints in heaven.

In some cases their faith also was focused on a coming Redeemer; but generally their concept of what that Redeemer was going to do was very murky and more often than not laced with error. Not many had the clear insight of Simeon and Anna, who blessed Jesus in His infancy (Luke 2:25-38). The majority had to wait until they were in Sheol—the place of the dead—to learn of the true ground for their eternal salvation, that it was not in the blood of animals which they had shed but in the blood of Christ.

But what of those under Jesus' personal ministry, before Calvary? Perhaps two brief case studies will be helpful.

Zacchaeus and the Thief

What did Zacchaeus believe that prompted Jesus to say, "Today salvation has come to this house" (Luke 19:9)? It is not likely that Zacchaeus would have repented to the point of giving half his goods to the poor and offering to make fourfold restitution, without being asked, if he had not been sure Jesus was the Messiah, and the only one who could meet his spiritual need There may also be a clue in Jesus' addendum: "because this man, too, is a son of Abraham"—the father of those who are justified by faith in the promise of God (Romans 4:1-3, et al.).

Perhaps what most commended him to Jesus was his intense desire to see Him, great enough for him to be willing to make a "monkey" out of himself. Actually, there was something comical yet deeply moving in the sight of this man, too short to see Jesus as one of the crowd, shinning up the tree and clinging precariously to the branches while peering down, eager to get a glimpse of this wonderful Prophet from Galilee. Whatever arrogance or social pride or personal dignity might have governed him normally was shed in this reckless quest. Doubtless no one was more surprised—or delighted—when Jesus looked up and said, "Zacchaeus make haste and come down, for today I must stay at your house" (Luke 19:5).

While his despised occupation as a tax gatherer did not disqualify him from Jesus' grace, his humility, openness, honesty, and willingness to make restitution testified to the kind of faith which justified Jesus in saying "Today salvation has come to this house."

As for the thief on the cross, there is no more astonishing, or instructive, demonstration of saving faith than that exhibited by this man. "Jesus," he said, "remember me when you come into your kingdom" (Luke 23:42, NASB). If we ask what doctrines he believed before joining Jesus in paradise, the answer is, plenty. Perhaps he could not have expressed his faith in formal dogmatic statements, but the doctrinal substance was there, nevertheless.

In some manner he had gotten hold of the fundamental truths which comprise the gospel. Here was a dying, crucified thief speaking to another dying victim of crucifixion expressing a sublime insight into the realities of the situation, so exactly opposite from appearances. He addressed Jesus as a Victor, not a victim. In some remarkable intuition he perceived that this Man's crucifixion was not final. It was not the terminus of either the Man or His mission, but a way-station to a kingdom.

Who did he think this man was? While the name "Jesus" (Saviour, both NASB and NIV) was common in those days, his use of the name demonstrated some knowledge of Him, perhaps even an awareness that in His case the name was crucially significant. His utter confidence that Jesus had a kingdom implied a recognition of Him as a king. And he declared his faith that in spite of the cross He would yet come into that kingdom; He would come into it in full power and the full possession of

His faculties—hence the request, "Remember me."

It is very possible this thief had at some time during the previous three years been in the crowds listening to Jesus. He might even have pushed into the inner circle and heard His prediction of His death and resurrection. While the disciples refused to listen to such unwelcome announcements, this man may have pondered, until now in the very happening he was able to piece it all together and understand. It is at least likely that his faith extended beyond the certainty of a kingdom to some degree of understanding that this cross was part of the essential scenario for the winning of that kingdom.

We cannot pass over the significance of the frame of mind which prompted this prayer and confession of faith. Before the faith affirmation he confessed his sins. When the other criminal "blasphemed" Jesus, this man "rebuked him." Then he added, "We indeed [are punished] justly, for we receive the due reward of our deeds; but this Man has done nothing wrong" (v. 41). No self-defense here, no maudlin self-pity, no projection of blame, but only total honesty, humility, and repentance. This is the only spiritual soil out of which saving faith can spring.

It should be noted that this thief did not ask Jesus to work a miracle and spare him the agony of the cross. He had the decency to admit that he was getting only what he deserved. But he begged Jesus to remember him later. A *thief* in the kingdom? What audacity! Not if his understanding included the faith that in some way this King was making provision for his eternal life in spite of his ill-desert! Here, hanging helplessly on a Roman cross, was exhibited some degree of perception that this Other Cross was redemptive. This certainly did not imply a full-blown doctrine of the Atonement, but it is hard to escape the conviction that at the heart of this man's faith was a true intuition that in some way this Jesus' death was related to his own salvation as its means.

The Normative Faith Standard

Zacchaeus and the dying chief are unique cases, yet they illustrate the underlying principles of any proper approach to Jesus. After the Resurrection and the Day of Pentecost the faith-way began to be more precisely spelled out. There are three passages we are justified in considering (two in this chapter), all of which either specify or imply concrete doctrinal confessions without which faith is not yet either normative or adequate.

The *first* is Paul and Silas' answer to the terrified Philippian jailer's question, "Sirs, what must I do to be saved?" The answer was: "Believe on the Lord Jesus Christ, and you will be saved" (Acts 16:30-31). Certainly they meant, "Put your trust in the Lord Jesus," for faith can never be saving until it becomes trust. But again we are faced with the need for substance. Trust cannot be put into a cognitive blank. The disciples were directing this man to put their trust into a person, who had a name—"the Lord Jesus Christ." But this was more than a name, it was a title: *the Lord Jesus Christ*—the Saviour who is both Lord and Christ.[1]

The jailer had just addressed them, *kurioi,* lords. Whether in his pagan ignorance and superstition he had mistaken the identity of these men because of the earthquake, and supposed the gods were before him, as in the case of the pagans in Lystra (Acts 14:11f), we do not know; but in any case Paul and Silas forestalled such a misplaced faith by saying, "No—believe in Jesus, who is the true Lord." At any rate a theological face was soon put to the name, for the disciples "spoke the word of the Lord to him and to all the others in his house: (v. 32). Before daybreak there was a happy baptizing, and "he rejoiced, having believed in God with all his household" (v. 34).

The disciples had not told the man to "believe in God," but to believe in "the Lord Jesus." But to believe in Him, he learned, was to *believe in God*. And so it is. Here is essential content for saving faith![2]

A *second* significant faith-salvation passage is in Paul's discussion of the faith-way of righteousness as it specifically relates to the Jews, in Romans 10:10, 11. Determined to "establish their own" righteousness, they miss the righteousness which "comes from God" (10:3, NIV). As a means to righteousness, Christ is the "end of the law," and becomes by His cross the source of a new righteousness available simply by believing in what Christ has done. Whereas the legal righteousness has this rule: "The man who does those things shall live by them," the evangelical righteousness through Christ has a different rule, the rule of "faith" (v. 6).

And faith truly is simple. It does not demand reenactments of dramatic proofs or revelations, by saying, "'Who will ascend into heaven?' (this is, to bring Christ down from above) or, 'Who will descend into the abyss?' (that is, to bring Christ up from the dead)" (vv. 6, 7). Rather, the faith-way of the Gospel is to accept without reservation the identity of Jesus and the truth of the resurrection. The word is "that if you confess with your mouth the Lord Jesus and believe in your heart that God has raised Him from the dead you will be saved." Saving faith does not anticipate some dramatic event about to happen, but fastens upon a dual event which has already happened—the Incarnation and the Resurrection. It is the crucified One who is *Lord*, as evidenced by the Resurrection.

Faith acknowledges that Jesus as Lord has already come from heaven, and He has already been raised from the dead—these are finished, historical facts. All faith has to do is stake everything on these facts. Confess Jesus openly as Lord (at whatever risk, even in Rome where Caesar claimed to be "lord") and believe inwardly that Jesus is alive—meaning His *identity is verified, His death is vindicated, its atoning efficacy validated, and His total victory assured.*

"Jesus is Victor!" is the elated watchword of the believer. This is the faith which assures salvation. And it is a kind of faith which *"is near you, in your mouth and in your heart"* (v. 8). We need seek no supporting miracles or comforts or philosophic props, but right where we are, as we are, we can put our whole trust in Jesus Christ the crucified, living Lord.

> *Just as I am, without one plea,*
> *But that Thy blood was shed for me,*
> *And that Thou bidst me come to Thee,*
> *O Lamb of God, I come, I come!*
> —Charlotte Elliott

Endnotes

1. Other versions follow the most authoritative Greek texts by eliminating "Christ"—a term which would convey little or no meaning to the jailer. But the title then would be, "The Saviour who is Lord."

2. We cannot be sure what the jailer had in mind by being "saved." It is not likely he was worried about either his head or his job, for a jailer who loses not a single prisoner in an earthquake has little to fear in that direction. It is more likely that a long simmering spiritual hunger was erupting. In any case not only the means of salvation was explained but the concept of salvation itself was corrected and enlarged before the night was over.

Chapter Five
The Gospel According to John 3:16

THE *THIRD* PASSAGE WHICH contributes to our understanding of what is to be believed if faith is to issue in salvation, is the Bible's best known and most loved verse, John 3:16—"For God so loved the world that He gave His only begotten Son, that whoever believes in Him should not perish but have everlasting life."

Almost all English speaking readers of John 3:16 would have some general understanding of what the verse is saying. Fortunately we are not in the predicament of the Dani tribe in the Baliem Valley of Irian Jaya to whom Myron Bromley went as a linguistic missionary in 1954. In trying to make this verse meaningful Bromley was frustrated at every turn, for he could find no word in their language for "God," "believe," or "everlasting life." Neither did they have a conception of sin, so could have no idea of an atonement by which they could be saved from sin. But he kept trying and gradually the Holy Spirit got through with sufficient enlightenment that belbeliefecame possible, in spite of what seemed to be insurmountable communication barriers. By 1961 the Christian and Missionary Alliance could report some eight thousand believers in more than twenty churches. There is clearly something about this verse which sooner or later strikes the inner chord of the human condition and answers to spiritual hunger.[1]

If some portions of this chapter seem difficult, may the reader remember the Danis, and keep plugging. Following the argument will be worth the effort, for it is centrally germane to the true nature of atonement and forgiveness.

Doctrinally Loaded

Nothing is more bland or doctrinally imprecise than this verse, as typically recited by Christians. "Just believe in Jesus, that's all, and you will be saved!" The implication is that there is nothing cognitive here for the mind to lay hold of. That many have touched Jesus by simple faith in the Name, with very little understanding, is no doubt true; but deep within them has been some perception of *Who He Is* and *What He Did,* even though dim, and beyond their ability to articulate.

But a close look at the verse and its context will correct any notion that the passage is non-doctrinal. Can believing "in him" mean any less than acknowledging Him as God's "one and only Son"? (NIV). And is not Jesus implying that believing in Him includes believing in Him as God's appointed means of not perishing? And does this not imply an awareness of "perishing"? Only people who come to the discovery of their lostness can believe in a Saviour from it.

And does not believing in him imply some concept of "eternal life"? To believe in Him intelligently rather than blindly is to say: "Jesus Christ is God's One and Only Son, God gave His Son because He loved the entire world, and desired everyone to be saved. If I believe in Him—who He is and what He was given for—then I will escape perishing—which means total and eternal lostness—and receive the gift of eternal life."

But there is yet a deeper note implied here. Can we believe savingly in Jesus without some grasp of what is meant by "gave"—He *gave* His one and only Son. That this divine *giving* is not primarily defined by the Incarnation is made clear by the context. Jesus had just said: "And as Moses lifted up the serpent in the wilderness, even so must the Son of Man be lifted up, that whoever believes in Him should not perish but have eternal life" (John 3:14-15). Here is the *death* of Jesus, as the antitype of the serpent, believe in Him *as the Lifted-up-One*, whose lifting was God's appointed means of turning back the divine judgment in the wilderness (Numbers 21:5-9).

Right here, then, in this best known discourse, we have an unmistakable declaration of a doctrine of Atonement, and this is included in what it means to "believe in him." If there is no perception of the Atonement in our faith it is not the kind of faith by which we "will not perish," or be given "eternal life."

Zacchaeus represents the multitudes who before Calvary grasped by faith only a portion of Jesus' identity and mission: it was a trust in Jesus to the extent that the light had been made available to them. But if and when genuine, it was subconsciously anticipatory, so that when Christ died and rose again, Zacchaeus and all like him found in this Living Lord the perfect consummation of hope and trust. Though their faith was initially incomplete in its objective content, it was nevertheless, as far as it went, entirely true. But as we, this side of Calvary, approach Christ, our faith cannot stop with the understanding of Zacchaeus. It must embrace the whole Gospel—Christ was "lifted up" for our redemption.

Typical of a conversion which has in it a solid cognitive element is that of Paul M. Anderson, a professor of biochemistry. He reports that for years he stumbled over the identity of Jesus Christ. "I intellectually accepted the idea of God, but I could not accept Jesus Christ," he says. But he came across *The Greatest Thing in the World* by Henry Drummond, and three shorhort sences awakened him: "Willpower does not change men. Time does not change men. Christ does." He turned to his wife and said, "Hey, that's it!" Later the reading of *Surprised by Joy* by C. S. Lewis helped him further. Then, "Suddenly I understood. Before I had seen Jesus Christ only as a man. Now I understood that Jesus Christ is the 'visible expression of the invisible God' who came to earth to live, but was put to death on the cross as a sacrifice that we might be saved from our sins." When he read in the Phillips translation the words of Paul, "The preaching of the cross is, I know, nonsense to those who are involved in this dying world, but to us who are being saved from that death it is nothing less than the power of God," he thought, "I understand that." And he adds, "Since that time I have had a sense of purpose and meaning in my life and work."[2]

Sin and Serpent

Just as the wilderness serpent sheds light on the meaning of the word "gave" in John 3:16, so do God's instructions to the Israelites clarify the meaning of the word "believes in Him." As the poet has said, it was literally "life for a look." Believing is looking. With us it is looking on Jesus the crucified, seeing in Him the antitype of the serpent, the One who bears our sin and God's wrath on our sin. It must be a look which acknowledges the justice of it all, and sees the propriety of wrath.

Furthermore, the inherent moral issues of the situation would demand that it be a look of true penitence, including a total surrender of the hostility toward God which had brought upon us such punishment. To attempt to appropriate the healing power of the serpent while clinging to the unbelief and rebellion would be not only hypocritical but utterly futile. God reads the heart too well for that.

But it must also be a look of faith, which accepts the pronouncement that the God who sent the serpents of judgment has now erected His archetypal Serpent, whose death on the cross can staunch the flow of the serpents' venom.

But before the look—speaking of the Israelites—could bring healing it had to bring deliverance from the wrath. The serpents were God's response to their *sin*. Their fully responsible unbelief and rebellion was the cause; serpent bites were punishments. So a look of faith was a look which saw in that serpent an escape from further punishment. The plague would be stopped. Healing was in the look, but forgiveness came first. Justification must ever underlie sanctification.

The look also was an act of obedience. For people hurting and dying from snake bites, looking at a replica on a pole would make no sense at all—absolutely none. But Moses told them to look because this was God's order. They finally were in such a state of fear and desperation that for once they would do anything God through Moses told them to do. But in their obedience was capitulation. They could not look and go on grumbling. In looking they surrendered.

But their looking was optional. Probably some stubbornly refused to look—refused to surrender to God and to Moses—and died. In the final tally personal freedom remains inviolate. So likewise the sinner and Christ. His death avails for the "whosoever who believeth in him," but the believing must be an act not only of accepting what God offers but coming on God's terms.

For a doctrine of the Atonement the significance of this is like a continental divide God's *provision* is complete; its *efficacy* is provisional. It rests with human choice, to believe or not to believe.

At Athens, following Paul's sermon, "Some of them sneered, but others...believed" (Acts 17:32, 34 NIV). To suppose that this diversity of response was pre-decreed by God, individually and personally, is to make a mockery of divine sovereignty and reduce the whole event to a charade. The individual will, while *influenced* by the pleading Spirit, and *enabled* by the Spirit, remains in control, both in the surrender and in the rebellion. To say that this makes salvation of man rather than of God is patently absurd. As some Lutherans say, "No man can save himself, but he can damn himself."

Faith and Atonement

We need to bear down further on the *provisional* nature of the Atonement. Jesus as God's serpent does not draw into Himself sin's venom in such a way that all who are bitten by sin are automatically delivered from its death-dealing power and eternal consequences, anymore than the mere act of creating a pole with the serpent on it instantly healed all in Israel. Rather it *became* God's appointed means of healing for all and only all who chose to look. So Christ's saving power is blocked by unbelief. It *becomes* personally efficacious for us one by one and only when we believe one by one. Our faith turns God's provision into an experiential personal salvation. Otherwise it remains mere provision. And so the Word: "Whom God set forth to be a propitiation by His blood, through faith" (Romans 3:25). No faith, no benefit. And the faith is not infused as an electric current animates a toy. It is our faith, exercised freely by us by choice. Believing is that which we choose to do.[3]

What Romans 3:25 says is simply this: As final as Christ's atoning work was, and as sufficient as it was, it remains an incomplete circle of redemption until the circle is closed by faith. It is the sinner's faith—both his belief and his trust—that turns Christ's death into a personally received atonement. As J. Kenneth Grider puts it: "His righteous wrath has now been propitiated by our permitting Christ's atonement to be applied to us personally."[4] If we do not appropriate it by faith God's wrath remains on us, as truly as if Christ had not died—for "he who does not believe the Son shall not see life, but the wrath of God abides on him" (John 3:36).

Apart from the sinner's upreach of faith the Atonement remains complete in the abstract, but concretely ineffectual. Available but not yet experienced Just as it took an act of faith in Egypt for the blood to be applied to the "two doorposts and on the lintel" (Exodus 12:7), and just as the promise of escape was dependent not only on shedding the blood but on this individual, deliberate act of *applying* it ("When I see the blood, I will pass over you"), so God personalizes the atonement in Christ only when we appropriate the blood for ourselves by a personal act of faith. Paul reconfirms this basic law of saving faith in v. 26b—"so as to be just and the one who justifies those who have faith in Jesus."

And the kind of faith which will bring Him into our hearts is a total abandonment of all other props. There must be a complete turning away from law as a means of salvation, of religious rites (as such), from other saviors, from all human philosophies, and certainly from every vestige of self-righteousness, as any ground whatsoever for the hope of salvation. Christ, and Christ's shed blood alone, is the Hope to which our faith clings and on whom it rests.

> *Rock of Ages, cleft for me,*
> > *Let me hide myself in Thee;*
> *Let the water and the blood,*
> > *From Thy wounded side which flowed,*
> *Be of sin the double cure,*
> > *Save from wrath and make me pure.*

> *Could my tears forever flow,*
> > *Could my zeal no languor know,*
> *These for sin could not atone—*
> > *Thou must save, and Thou alone;*
> *In my hand no price I bring,*
> > *Simply to Thy cross I cling.*
> > > —Augustus M. Toplady

Endnotes

1. Ruth A. Tucker, *Sacred Stories* (Grand Rapids, MI: Zondervan Publishing House, 1989), p. 143.
2. "A Scientist's Search for God," by Paul M. Anderson, in *Reasons To Be Glad* (Excerpts from *Decision* magazine, compiled by the editors; Billy Graham Evangelistic Association), pp. 176-77.
3. In the words of Jack Wright: "It is not the belief of a student studying a problem, but a drowning man grabbing a life-line, believing it will save him." Comment to the author.
4. *Wesleyan Holiness Theology*, an unpublished systematic theology, ms p. 844. (In process of publication by the Beacon Hill Press of Kansas City.)

Chapter Six
The Elements of Saving Faith

IN SEEKING TO GAIN further insight into the nature of faith, we need, at the very outset, to be reminded that the term "saving faith" does not mean that faith itself has the power to save, or bears any merit by which salvation is earned. Faith is rather the hand that reaches up to the outstretched hand of God's unmerited favor. It is the humility which receives salvation as a free gift. But faith has in it certain qualities without which it is not real but a pretense—a counterfeit thing which, like a rubber wire, is powerless to channel the current of saving grace.

Moral Earnestness

The fundamental element is sincerity. For faith to avoid hypocrisy, as well as utter impotence, it must have at its core a profound desire to receive what Christ died to provide. This means that an intellectual belief in certain doctrines, no matter how correct the doctrines may be, will not alter one's direction or destiny one whit; for the beliefs have not yet taken control of the heart.

The spirit must be awakened to sin and begin to feel, in some authentic measure, not only the horror and shame of it, but a longing to be free from it. Then when the gospel breaks upon the mind every fiber of the being will reach up to grasp *this*—salvation from sin. Sin is the disease; hell is only a by-product. To fear hell without fearing sin, to want to believe in order to be saved from hell while secretly holding on to sin, is to be deceived by the chicanery of one's own heart. It is to mock God who has provided at infinite cost the cure for the disease. Equally monstrous is it to profess Christ and become sentimental about Him, yet be trifling with the sin that cost Him His blood.

Surely it is obvious that to desire to be saved from sin is to be willing, indeed passionately anxious, to turn away from it. This is why John the Baptist, Jesus Himself, and all the apostles universally preached repentance. The order was always: Repent, and then believe.[1] Without repentance the attempt to believe will be abortive and any profession of religion will be spurious.

The nature of faith is such that a spirit of penitence is a constituent element. While it may be possible to repent without believing, it is impossible to believe without repenting. While the one dying thief believed unto salvation, the other did not. How could he, when in his heart there was no repentance? We have learned very little from the New Testament if we suppose that saving faith can coexist with bitter impenitence.

Or from the Old Testament, either, for that matter. After declaring to Israel that the Lord required of them

> *But to do justly,*
> *To love mercy,*
> *And to walk humbly with their God,*
>   —(Micah 6:8)

He almost immediately adds:

> *Shall I count pure those with the wicked scales,*
> *And with the bag of deceitful weights?* (v. 11).

Are we to believe that in some moral sleight of hand the Atonement annuls this, so that if "in Christ" we can continue with our dishonest scales and false weights with impunity? That the blood of Christ hides our trickery from the Father's eyes? Any such concept of the Atonement is an insult to the blood (if not sheer blasphemy) and a slander on a holy God. Such an atonement would be immoral at the core.

Repentance is a facing of sin. When we have done that we will be capable of seeing the gospel as the answer to our sin. Only then does believing become possible.

Believing the gospel is the end to which repentance leads, and repentance is that on which believing is predicated.

Faith and "Works"

Furthermore, neither John the Baptist, Jesus, nor Paul hesitated to impose "works" on persons professing to want to repent. When the crowd asked John the Baptist "What should we do then?" he told the selfish people to begin to share, the tax collectors to quit their extortion, and the soldiers to be honest and be content with their pay (Luke 3:10-14)

When the rich young ruler came to Jesus asking what he must "do" to inherit eternal life, Jesus did not say to him, "Just believe, that's all: you don't need to do a thing!" Rather, He specified *plenty* to do, and said, "Then come, follow me" (Matthew 19:15-22). The young man would have learned by and by that his obedience did not provide the ultimate ground for his salvation; but also that he could not get on justifying ground without it. It was not because Jesus was unwilling to save him that he went away sorrowful, but because he was unwilling to *act*, to *do* what he was told to do. He wo wouldot tear himself away from *things* in order to become one with Christ.

Paul was equally adamant that true repentance involved "works." He testified to King Agrippa that he was not disobedient to the Lord's commission to "turn [sinners] from darkness to light, and from the power of Satan unto God," but preached everywhere "that they should repent, turn to God, and do works befitting repentance" (Acts 26:18-20). Without turning there is no forgiveness, and turning is repenting, the kind of repenting that gladly makes restitution where possible, and makes whatever other adjustments and changes are necessary to conform to the requirements of the Christian life.

We are not to infer that all of these "works" must be *completed* before God will forgive. But God must see in the heart a willingness to do whatever "getting right with God" requires, when and as the details are seen. The exhortation "Be reconciled to God" (2 Corinthians 5:20) implies this much.

While the impediment to reconciliation consisting of our past sins has been provisionally removed by God in Christ, our being reconciled to God demands the removal, as far as it lies within our power, of those things which constitute an ongoing barrier, and which would make true reconciliation morally impossible. A rebel against the king who seeks reconciliation while secretly holding on to his weapons of rebellion is trying to wrest the benefit of reconciliation without playing fair. Let us avoid all such trickery with God An earthly king might be fooled, but not our Heavenly King.

Prodigals and Sheep

In helping us understand the true doctrine of "works" the parable of the Prodigal Son is instructive also. Ultimately it was by grace he was saved; but it was the kind of grace that waited patiently for the son to come to himself, to arise, and make his humble, penitent way back to the father's house. Without action on the son's part he would have rotted in the pig pen, in spite of his father's love. His father respected the boy's freedom as a moral agent. And he was too wise to make any futile attempt to force a rebel home who was not yet through with his rebellion.

For some it is more comforting to think of the earlier parable in the chapter (Luke 15) as normative, not the Prodigal Son. In this story the shepherd seeks the sheep until he finds it; he does not wait at home until it voluntarily returns. This is the way we prefer to think of our spiritual security: if we wander, the Shepherd will find us and bring us back again. So we need not worry, or exercise any personal concern, or put forth any effort. Comforting, but misleading. The purpose of the parable is not to teach doctrine about the salvation of persons, but to shame the Pharisees who were carping about Christ's eating with sinners. If they would seek a lost sheep, shouldn't He seek lost sinners? But He sought them as responsible human beings, not as dumb creatures.

Since, however, the shepherd-sheep motif is so prominent in the Bible—as would be expected in a pastoral culture—we are justified in pausing a moment to look more closely. Human beings do, because of sinfulness, have some sheep-like characteristics, such as the tendency to stray (Isaiah 53:6). Furthermore, *we need* a shepherd's care (Psalm 23). "Feed my sheep," Jesus commanded Peter (John 21:15-17).

But the analogy soon breaks down. No four-legged, woolly, bleating sheep will be at the Judgment, but *we* will. For sheep are not *persons* whose wanderings are sinful and blameworthy.

How wonderfully true it is that Jesus seeks the lost! That is what He came into the world to do. But He seeks them as intelligent beings, created in His image, who are both responsible and accountable. He does not seek them as hapless, innocent animals, who stray without intending to, or even being aware that they are straying. He seeks them by teaching them, dying for them, and drawing them by His Spirit; but He does not arbitrarily carry them back to the flock on His shoulder when they have chosen to stray and prefer to be left alone.

This does not mean that the Spirit ceases to strive with wandering Christians, or does not seek to recover them by hedging providences. But the lovely picture of a shepherd just reaching down and picking up a lost sheep does not fit the case. When a backslider is called a "lost sheep" quote marks must be put around the words. It is a figure of speech. The reality is that here is a person, free agent, who can respond to the Shepherd's overtures or reject them.[2]

Furthermore, Jesus put an identifying mark on those whom He acknowledged as His sheep: "My sheep listen to my voice; I know them, and they follow me" (John 10:27). If we are spiritual vagabonds we have no claim to sheephood.

So the parable of the Prodigal is more normative, after all. To get back to the Father's house the sinner must make a decision, and say, "I will arise and go."

Endnotes

1. Cf. Mark 1:15; 6:12; Luke 13:3, 5: Acts 2:38; 3:19; 8:22; 17:20; 20:21; 26:20, *et al.*
2. Cf. Matthew 18:12-14, where recovering the lost sheep is problematic—not "when he finds it" but "if he finds it" (cf. NASB).

Chapter Seven
This Matter of Lordship

EQUALLY INTRINSIC TO SAVING faith is submission to Christ. To believe in the Lord Jesus is to believe in Jesus as Lord. This means to believe in His right to rule. For me to believe in that right is for me to believe in His right to rule *me*. But how can that mental belief bring about my salvation unless I acknowledge that right, not just with my lips but in my heart, and with all my being yield to it? I must embrace and accept what that lordship means, or I am still a rebel. And to suppose that a sinner can be forgiven while still a rebel is to turn all morality on its head.

When our Lord taught us to pray,

> *Your will be done*
> *On earth as it is in heaven* (Matthew 6:10)

did He intend for us to say it muttering under our breath, "everywhere, Lord, but in me"?

We need to look again at the terms of reconciliation. When the Word says, "We implore you on Christ's behalf, be reconciled to God" (2 Corinthians 5:21) we are to see in this a plea t lay down our weapons of rebellion and surrender to God: to accept the reconciliation He has provided in Christ, *on His terms*. Reconciliation, by definition, is not a mere truce or a secret pretense for advantage, but the restoration of harmonious relations. When that reconciliation is between God and sinners, it is not between equals. Rather it is a reconciliation of a son to his Father, of a creature to his Creator, of a redeemed person to his Redeemer, and of a subject to his Sovereign. Hence reconciliation is impossible without the surrender of one's will, and full capitulation to God's sovereign rights. Otherwise, the Garden rebellion still goes on.

Faith and Obedience

Obedience naturally follows surrender; thus obedience also can be named as a constituent element of saving faith. This is proving the sincerity of our choice of Christ as Lord. "Lordship and obedience are correlative terms," says William M. Greathouse.[1] Obedience is simply the acting out of a new relationship. This connection between faith and obedience is so inseverable that Dietrich Bonhoeffer was entirely Biblical when he said "He who believes is he who obeys and he who obeys is he who believes."[2]

"It would be strange...." observes Alistair Begg, "to bear allegiance to Jesus Christ, and then live my life disregarding what would please Him. [But] some do, because they think that lordship is a spe8Xspeciakage which they have decided not to choose. But there is only one package. It is confrontation with Christ and conformity to Christ."[3]

The logical connection is apparent in the fact that faith includes not only an acknowledgment of God's sovereignty but a trust in His love and wisdom. What kind of "trust" would it be that knew God's will and proceeded to reject it? The faith that brings into the heart the love of God, "poured out...by the Holy Spirit" (Romans 5:5) brings in this love a profound desire to please God and a ready acceptance of His will in all things. The obedience therefore is not a wooden legalism or fear-driven servitude but a joyous disposition—the outgrowth of a profound commitment to obey God because we are devoted to Him. To try to sever living faith from obedience is to drain from faith its vitality and reality. It is to play games and deal in fictions.

The indissoluble unity of faith and obedience is illustrated by the reference to the Israelites in the letter to the Hebrews. Drawing lessons from the rebellion of the Israelites in the wilderness the writer says: "Beware, brethren, lest there be in any of you an evil heart of unbelief in departing from the living God" (Hebrews 3:12). Unbelief and turning away are correlative. By implication, the correlative of belief is not turning away.

Further: "And to whom did He swear that they would not enter His rest, but to them who did not obey? So we see that they could not enter in because of unbelief" (Hebrews 3:18-19). Again, faith and obedience are correlative. Their disobedience was an expression of unbelief. True belief would have obeyed. They had covenanted to serve this righteous and holy God, who had worked miracles before their eyes and brought them out of Egypt. But their faith in Him was not strong enough to believe that He could make them successful in conquering Canaan. Because they did not believe they would not obey. This is forever the order. Every act of disobedience is a proof of disbelief. Disbelief is sin, and sin brings death.

The writer proceeds with his application and exhortation: "Therefore, since a promise remains of entering His rest, let us fear lest any of you seem to have come short of it. For indeed the gospel was preached to us as well as to them; but the word which they heard did not profit them, not being mixed with faith in those who heard it" (Hebrews 4:1-2); i.e., the *kind of faith which obeys.* And no other kind is worth a farthing.

No Obedience, No Salvation

There are at least three passages which incontrovertibly deny any possibility of ultimate salvation without obedience. One is Matthew 7:21: "Not everyone who says to me, 'Lord, Lord,' will enter the kingdom of heaven, but he who does the will of My Father in heaven." Here are people who suppose that creed will exempt them from deed, that obeisance will take the place of obedience, and that grace excludes works, including doing the will of God. These imagine that piously addressing Jesus as Lord will suffice for making Him Lord. But Jesus' verdict is inescapable: no obedience, no kingdom.

Another unbendable verse is Hebrews 5:9. Jesus, having perfected (qualified) Himself by His own obedience all the way, "became the author of eternal salvation for all who obey Him." This is preset tense, implying ongoing obedience as the rule of life. The notion that one initial act of obedience will cover a subsequent pattern of disobedience is foolishness. "For if I build again those things which I destroyed, I make myself a transgressor" (Galatians 2:18). The verdict of these verses is clear: No continuing obedience, no continuing salvation.

The third pivotal passage is 1 John 2:4: "He who says, 'I know Him,' and does not keep His commandments, is a liar, and the truth is not in him." There is no exegesis or "eisegesis" which can blunt this sharp declaration. Here is the big talker again, like the former "Lord, Lord" person, whose profession is not only empty but impudent. Ultimately he will find himself among all the other liars (Revelation 21:8, 27; 22:15). C. S. Lewis is quoted as saying: "In this world are two classes of people—those who say to God, 'Thy will be done,' and those to whom God says, 'Thy will be done.'"

We are seeking to analyze the kind of faith which is meant by the Protestant principle of *sola fides* at least Biblically understood. What do we find? Simply that if we abstract from faith repentance, surrender, and obedience, no faith remains.

Saving Faith and Discipleship

The bifurcation of salvation and discipleship, that is, the popular notion that sinners can by an act of faith bring themselves once for all under the security of the Blood, then later decide to become disciples (or decide not to), cannot be suststai Biblically. In that case the Great Commission is not directed to getting people saved but only to making disciples—*with baptism contingent upon their becoming disciples.* "Go therefore and make disciples of all the nations, baptizing them in the name of the Father and of the Son and of the Holy Spirit, teaching them to observe all things that I have commanded you" (Matthew 28:19-20).

If the discipleship which observes all that Jesus commanded could be separated from salvation, it would then be proper to say, "Have you accepted Christ as your Saviour?" "Yes, I have. I'm not afraid to die any more because I have been told I am unconditionally secure." "Very good; now if you will just decide to become a disciple also, and become willing to obey all of Christ's commands, we will baptize you." This drives a wedge between saving faith and discipleship, with water baptism being reserved as the badge of discipleship. The absurdity is sufficient refutation.

Discipleship is spelled out by Jesus in His challenge: "If anyone desires to come after Me, let him deny himself, and take up his cross daily [not just once, or by spurts, or experimentally, or temporarily], and follow Me" (Luke 9:23). He must renounce his self-sovereignty, accept whatever for him the cost may be to follow Jesus, and proceed to follow Jesus as a lifetime commitment. Jesus proceeds to pin on this eternal destiny. "For whoever desires to save his life will lose it, but whoever loses his life for My sake will save it. For what profit is it to a man if he gains the whole world, and is himself destroyed or lost?" (vv. 24-25). If we just revert in wording to the old-fashioned term "soul" (KJV), and remember that winning men to Christ is "saving souls," we will see how impossible it is to suppose Jesus is talking about a kind of optional discipleship unrelated to personal salvation.

Recently a prominent radio preacher was seeking to explain the difference between being a Christian and a disciple. He used this confrontation in Caesarea Philippi as recorded in Matthew 15:13-26.[4] The speaker established that Peter was a Christian by referring to his confession: "You are the Christ, the Son of the living God." But he "proved" the difference between being a Christian and a disciple by verse 24: "If anyone desires to come after Me [become My disciple] let him deny himself, and take up his cross, and follow Me." Peter, and the others, were Christians but not yet disciples, the speaker concluded.

This strained and artificial disjunction between salvation and discipleship is easily disproved. In the first place, the Twelve were consistently called disciples from the first (Matthew 4:1, et al.). In the second place, when Jesus called them "they forsook all, and followed him" (Luke 5:11; cf. Mark 1:15). Third, they testified to having "forsaken all" and Jesus confirmed their testimony (Matthew 19:27-29). In a sense, when they left family and lucrative trades behind in order to become a wandering band of learners, following Jesus everywhere He went and hanging on every word from His mouth, they were denying themselves and taking up their cross. Naturally they wouldn't have *called* their obedience "crossbearing," for until this conversation in Caesarea Philippi they had no concept of the cross principle. But to suppose that therefore up until this time they were "Christians" but not "disciples" is to manhandle the meaning of words.

Not an Option, but a Process

What is often overlooked is that while discipleship is a commitment implicit in any sound conversion, and consciously the full intention of anyone who sincerely comes to Jesus, the unfolding of discipleship is a process. This process includes both cognitive and spiritual advances. As a result there will be distinct stages in one's level of discipleship. Jesus at this point in teaching the disciples was beginning to acquaint them with the cross principle, both His own and theirs. This is understandably an unfolding comprehension. All disciples, no matter how eager and fervent, come from time to time to a better understanding of what their individual discipleship entails. This discourse on discipleship in Caesarea Philippi was a watershed revelation.

But progress in discipleship involves not only advances in intellectual perception but spiritual advances as well. Obedience must step up to the new insights. In the case of the disciples the matter remained murky and incomprehensible in their minds until after the resurrection, when Jesus cleared up many questions, and instructed them to settle down in Jerusalem to wait for the baptism with the Holy Spirit. When filled with the Spirit there was a burst of understanding far beyond any experienced before. They entered into a new spiritual dimension. But this was not the begi2Xeginni their discipleship; it was only the beginning of their life as fully sanctified disciples.

It is important to see that the discipleship undertaken by any sincere believer in Jesus is real, even though he or she struggles with sluggishness and dullness, and undercurrents of reluctance which surge at times to the surface and create spiritual conflict. This doesn't mean that the Christian is overtly rebelling, or trying to decide whether or not to "become a disciple"; it only means that he is experiencing normal spiritual adolescence because yet double-minded. His need is exactly what was the need of the Twelve (including Matthias)—to be baptized with the Holy Spirit. This will cleanse his heart from that lurking reluctance to face up to the full claims of Christ's lordship, and thereby immensely reconfirm and fortify his discipleship.

Summary

Sola fides is indeed the true doctrine. But the *fides* which touches God includes *fidelity*. The saying is credited to Luther: "It is faith alone that saves, but the faith that saves is not alone."[5] Faith without the works of obedience is still dead (James 2:26).

To attempt to extract from God eternal life by a kind of believing which does not carry with it a grateful and obedient spirit, and a commitment to please the One in whom we believe, is a kind of spiritual perjury—a pretense for gain, while hiding our cupidity and insincerity.

It is telling God He can have our "soul" for heaven while on earth we keep self to ourselves.

Paul spelled it out precisely: "The only thing that counts is faith expressing itself through love" (Galatians 5:6b, NIV). Faith that does not so express itself does not count. But love will obey God and live righteously with men.

It is imperative that we see the real state of the case here. We are not admitting that saving faith needs to be buttressed and strengthened, or even expressed, by repentance, surrender, and obedience. What is being declared, and what needs to be seen in utter clarity, is that these are the constituent elements of that faith which is the human response to the gospel, through which we experience salvation. Bleed faith at any point and it dies.

Whatever else we need then to say about the Atonement, its saving benefits are conditional, and the one, indispensable condition is faith—a Biblical faith. And it is as inherently as indispensable after conversion as it is the condition for conversion. Justifying faith does not extract the venom from disobedience and render it harmless.

Endnotes

1. "Romans," *Beacon Bible Commentary*, vol. 8, 33.
2. *The Cost of Discipleship* (New York: Macmillan Co., 1963), p. 69.
3. "Find Out What Pleases the Lord," by Alistair Begg, *Real People, Real Faith,* ed. by David Porter, The Keswick Convention Council (STL Books, Bromley, Kent, England, 1988), p. 187. Begg also quotes an oral statement made by John Stott: "There is only one standard, to live under the lordship of Jesus Christ. It is not an option."
4. Charles R. Swindoll.
5. Quoted by Begg, *Real People*, p. 188.

Chapter Eight
Who Can Believe?

HOW IS SAVING FAITH to be acquired? Before attempting an answer let us first remind ourselves that faith is the name we give to an action. Believing is the action. This consists of two parts, an intellectual perception of truth and a volitional response to truth. We believe something to be true and act accordingly. The sinner therefore perceives the gospel to be true, accepts it intellectually as true, then wills to act on the implications and demands of this truth.

That action includes coming to Christ in repentant prayer and consciously and deliberately accepting the offer of salvation. "Believe on the Lord Jesus Christ, and you will be saved" (Acts 16:31) is as true for the sinner today as it was for the Philippian jailer. But the believing must have in it, implicitly at least, all its constituent elements if it is to be valid and salvation is to be experienced.

When Faith is Blocked

The Bible teaches that this exercising of faith is not always possible. "How can you believe, who receive honor from on another, and do not seek the honor that comes from the only God?" (John 5:44). When we desire anything more than God we cannot believe for salvation.

Neither is faith in Jesus possible in the presence of disbelief in the Word; "If you believed Moses, you would believe Me" (v. 46). Jesus is implying that there were teachings in the writings of Moses which pointed to Him, and which if truly believed would have prompted them to believe in Him. They claimed to believe Moses; they cited him as their authority every day. But their faith was selective. They refused to believe in Moses anything which did not match their preconceptions of what the Messiah was supposed to be like and what He was supposed to do.

Also, love of sin will of course paralyze the faith faculty. "This is the condemnation," Jesus said, "that the light has come into the world, and men loved darkness rather than light because their deeds were evil" (John 3:19). The verdict is that love of darkness and faith in Christ are antithetical; one excludes the other.

Blocked by God?

But apart from these inherent moral impediments to faith, are there blockades erected by God Himself? To a mind untwisted by doctrinal bias such a question would seem outrageous. But it has to be raised for that is exactly the teaching of Calvinism. This system, as taught by John Calvin (1509-1564) and his followers, asserts that from eternity, before time and before the foundation of the world, God selected in advance those who should be saved. According to this doctrine, therefore, individual salvation is entirely a matter of God's election, and in no sense a matter of personal choice, i.e., a personal choice which is truly free. The choice may *seem* to be free, at the moment of conversion, but in reality the choice is pre-programmed, and implemented at that moment by the irresistible influences of the Holy Spirit.

In this scheme of things, faith is not truly an option, but a supernatural infusion. God the Spirit plants faith in the heart, a kind of faith which is thereafter indestructible and nonforfeitable. This is the teaching of all the major Calvinistic creeds, such as Westminster Confession, and such modern interpreters as Anthony Hoekema and Zane Hodges.[1]

According to this doctrine, therefore, the answer to the question, "Who can believe?" is, "Only the elect." The rest are shut out, locked up forever in their unbelief.

The Question of Sovereignty

There has developed in the general Calvinistic consciousness a deep fear of detracting from God's sovereignty, on the one hand, and detracting from God's glory, on the other, by seeming to give to human beings the slightest vestige of merit or credit for their own ultimate destiny. There is a knee-jerk horror of any degree of synergism (man working with God) in order to protect monergism (God alone the effective agent). Therefore the highly emotional outrage against any teaching which in such Calvinistic minds smacks of salvation by works.

Such thinking fails to see that the doctrine which makes God solely responsible for the saved also makes Him responsible for the lostness of the damned. How this can be to God's glory Calvinists fail to say.

Today moderate Calvinists are desperately anxious to squirm out of this implication. They reject so-called "double predestination," which is that the lostness of the finally unsaved is as predetermined by God as the redemption of the saved. The reasoning now has shifted to the fact that since all have sinned, no one deserves to be saved. That is, no one has a claim on God's mercy. And God is not under obligation to save anyone. Therefore if He chooses to save some it is pure benevolence, and He has "done no wrong" if He simply leaves the rest to bear the consequences of their sin, as they deserve.

It is put quite plausibly by Edward Fudge. In a valiant attempt to build a bridge between Calvinism and Arminianism he develops a series of couplet propositions, one set being:

> *Every accountable person deserves to be lost.*
> *No accountable person deserves to be saved.*

Then from these twin premises he draws a conclusion: "Every careful Calvinist insists that God deserves no blame for the fate of the lost."[2] But this is what logicians would call a *non sequitor* (it does not follow). The statement can be a logical inference from the premise *only if God uses the same means and exerts the same power to save all as He does to save some*.

The Calvinists build on a basic structure of ideas: some persons are marked out in advance as persons God designs to save; these persons are brought to salvation by the special and irresistible action of the Spirit upon their wills, reversing their direction, and precipitating repentance, faith, and obedience. Unless God so marked them and acted *upon* them they would be helpless to do anything about their salvation. The "unmarked," i.e., those who are passed by, are just left in their sins, to receive ultimately the due reward of their deeds. The logic of the contemporary moderate Calvinist is that since God is not responsible for their sins He is not responsible for the fact that they are not among the saved. This logic will not stand up, for God is responsible by default. The fact that He saves some, by irresistible means, proves that He could save everyone if He so chose; not to choose to do so is to become responsible for the fate of those He passes by. (More of this in the next chapter.)

Ephesians 1:4 will help us to see the gravity of the implications implicit in the idea of *one-sided* divine action. Here we read that God "chose us in Him [Christ] before the foundation of the world, that we should be holy and without blame before him in love." This is understood Calvinistically to be a sovereign choice of "us"—that is, some persons in distinction from the mass who are not so chosen.

But the "us" must not be detached from the purpose of the choice: "that we should be holy." To make the "we" selective is to imply that God desires some to be holy and is indifferent to the unholiness of others Can anyone seriously charge this on a holy God? Holiness which is indifferent to unholiness ceases to exist This would be like parents with six children: the parents want two of them to be pure and honest and obedient, but they are willing for the others to be impure and dishonest and disobedient. In that case we all know that the parents are themselves morally ambivalent and any pretense of concern one way or the other cannot but be window dressing. While such an anomaly might be found in earthly parents, sinful as they are, can we escape blasphemy if we attempt to pin such a charge on God? *This* dishonors God, not the allowance to man of a real option in his own destiny.

The simple and obvious meaning of the text is that since the Fall holiness is now available only in and through the Redeeming Christ, no longer in simple obedience to law (as in the Garden) or by virtue of inherited nature.

But if some would still insist that the divine choice is that only *some* are to be "in Him" (Christ), then we must answer by pointing to the plain teachings of the New Testament that Christ is offered to all and is available to all. But apart from the tenor of Scripture, one's moral sense knows that if it is intrinsic to divine holiness to require holiness, and if the required holiness is available only to those who are in Christ, to then erect barricades of eternal decrees which would keep some away from Christ would be to create a moral morass of contradictions, which sound thinking could not possibly ascribe to a holy God.

The Drawing of the Spirit

Admittedly it is not possible to exercise faith in Christ without the drawing of the Holy Spirit. Jesus said, "No man can come to Me unless the Father who sent Me draws him" (6:44). Total depravity means at least this much, that apart from prevenient grace sinners will not even desire to turn to Christ.

"Prevenient grace" is the grace that goes before; i.e., it is the grace which works in the hearts of men and women before conversion, drawing them to God in Christ. It is the action of the Spirit in awakening and convicting. This grace is a universal benefit of the Atonement, which reaches back to Adam and forward to the end of human history, making the human race salvable. And it is a grace which is extended to every person coming into the world. This creates the responsiveness in the human heart for the evangelistic appeal of the gospel.

Before Pentecost this grace was channeled primarily through law, providence, and conscience. Jesus taught that following the completion of His own redemptive ministry the Holy Spirit would be poured out in a new measure, and He would become the primary agent of the Father in drawing men and women. "And when He has come, He will convict the world of sin, of righteousness, and of judgment" (John 16:8). This is a universal ministry—not just to the "elect" but to "the world." Since no one can say, "I am not in the world," no one can say, "He passed me by."

And the essence of prevenient grace is that the "want to" is implanted in every heart, though not coercively or irresistibly, and not always in equal measure. Many have strongly felt the inner drawing, according to their own word, and experienced keep longings for God, but in the end turned away—as sadly as did the rich young ruler (Mark 10:22).

Furthermore, Jesus specified that people would be convicted "of sin, because they do not believe in Me" (v. 9). This means at least two things: First, every sin ever committed is gathered up into this one supreme sin of refusing to believe in Jesus. Second, it means that by not believing in Jesus people are forfeiting the only possible way out of their sin. But the note here is clearly a note of personal responsibility. They miss salvation because they freely choose not to believe.

Jesus declares personal responsibility also when He turns the coin over and explains, "Everyone who listens to the Father and learns from him comes to me" (John 6:45b, NIV). So we wear the shoe of responsibility after all. Because of prevenient grace, we can listen to the Father; that is, we can turn our attention to God and spiritual things, and begin to discover what God says in the Scripture, if we choose to. Such searching will lead one straight to faith in Jesus, if not aborted by stubborn impenitence.

Ephesians 2:4 stresses God's action in our salvation: "But because of his great love for us, God, who is rich in mercy, made us alive in Christ even when we were dead in transgressions" (NIV). But this must be balanced with Ephesians 5:14b:

> Wake up, O sleeper,
>   rise from the dead,
> and Christ will shine on you (NIV).

It needs to be seen that these two opposites do not even constitute a paradox. Rather they explain each other. All of salvation is of God, whose initiative makes salvation possible, and to whose mercy all can be ascribed. But His action is not mechanical, but works with the free response of the sinner who is exhorted to act; and the implication of the verse is that God extends to him all the power necessary so to act. The Holy Spirit stirs us out of our slumber, but in the process we can be said to "wake up," for we respond willingly. And unless we wake up and rise up out of the death of sin we have no legitimate expectation that "Christ will shine" on us.

And as for the universality of the drawing—whether or not God draws only the elect—Jesus uses the same word found in John 6:44, *helkuo* "to draw," in His promise: "And I, when I am lifted up from the earth, will draw all men to myself" (John 12:32).[3] All men are drawn, not just some.

There is no excuse therefore. While prevenient grace is needed, it is universally present. Only in the sense that ability to turn to God and believe is made possible as an unconditional benefit of the Atonement, and administered impartially by the Holy Spirit—only in this sense can faith be said to be a gift. The capacity is of grace, the believing is by choice.

The oft-quoted passage in support of the idea that faith is an infusion in passive, divinely selected recipients is: "For by grace you have been saved through faith, and that not of yourselves; it is the gift of God, not of works, lest anyone should boast" (Ephesians 2:8). But A. T. Robertson points out that "and this," *kai touto,* which is neuter, refers neither to faith nor grace, both of which are feminine, "but to the act of being saved by grace conditioned on faith on our part." He comments, "'Grace' is God's part, 'faith' ours."[4]

The general assumption of the Scripture is always that while the drawing of the Spirit is essential such drawing is neither irresistible nor selective; and that therefore believing for salvation is an option of which the sinner is ultimately responsible. The language cannot bear any other sense, as in Jesus' words to Nicodemus (to return to John 3): "For God did not send His Son into the world to condemn the world, but that the world through Him might be saved" (v. 17). This is declared to be God's purpose and desire—the salvation of the world, *all of it.*

Endnotes

1. According to the Westminster Confession, Chapter III, Section III: "By the decree of God, for the manifestation of his glory, some men and angels are predestinated unto everlasting life, and others foreordained to everlasting death.

"IV. These angels and men, thus predestinated and foreordained, are particularly and unchangeably designed; and their number is so certain and definite that it can not be either increased or diminished" (Philip Schaff, *The Creeds of Christendom* [Baker Book House, reprint 1969], III:608f. Hoekema endorses the Canons of Dort statement: "This elect number [those whom God has chosen from eternity], though by nature neither better nor more deserving than others,...God has decreed to give to Christ to be saved by Him, and effectually to call (*efficaciter vocare*) and draw them to His communion by Word and Spirit." *Saved By Grace,* p. 88.

2. "How Wide is God's Mercy?" *Christianity Today,* April 27, 1992, p. 32.

3. It is not incidental that the word used is *draw,* rather than *drag,* which would have been *suro.* Cf. John 21:6, 8, 11.

4. *Word Pictures in the New Testament,* 4:524.

Chapter Nine
God's Plan for All

THERE IS NO HINT in the Scriptures we have looked at so far of a secret election of *some* of the world. This would be a scandalous insinuation of insincerity in God and dishonesty in Jesus. Now, "He who believes in Him is not condemned; but he who does not believe is condemned already, because he has not believed in the name of the only begotten Son of God" (John 3:18). There are "whoevers" (NIV) on both sides, and the side is totally self-determined. *Anyone* may come to Jesus, *anyone* may refuse. Terrible option. But anything else would be puppetry. If selected persons are converted by an arbitrary act of God and infused with saving faith, they are robots and puppets, and there is absolutely no moral value in their reactions whatsoever. Such a salvation by such means would be to God's dishonor, not to His sovereign glory.

A Universal Call

Anthony A. Hoekema admits the universality of the gospel call but still clings to the doctrine of a limited atonement and secret efficacy of the call to the elect. He makes a valiant attempt to defend God against the charge of blatant insincerity which his position invites. He writes: "But we insist that we can hold to this well-meant gospel call while at the same time maintaining the doctrine of election and limited atonement."[1] He calls this a paradox, but it is hard to see how it is not rather a contradiction.

Hoekema says that some Hyper-Calvinists (his term) acknowledge the difficulty and solve it by stating flatly that since "the Bible teaches election and reprobation, it simply cannot be true that God desires the salvation of all to whom the gospel comes."[2] He rejects this way out but equally rejects the Arminian solution which postulates a prevenient grace operative toward all, making possible their salvation but which may individually be resisted. This, he says, "leaves us with a God who is not sovereign"[3] An astonishing statement indeed! Surely God is *sufficiently* sovereign to grant human beings freedom to reject His overtures if He chooses to. His sovereignty would be crippled if He could not.

We cannot harmonize such polarities. Sincerity in God's offer of salvation to all cannot meld with secret election and limited atonement. What would we think of the shipbuilder who professed ardent concern for the safety of all on board but deliberately provided lifeboats for only half?

Some nominal Calvinists who have abandoned the tenet of a limited atonement, and now say that Christ died for all, would protest this analogy. They would exclaim, "The shipbuilder *did* provide sufficient lifeboats for all!" But since they still cling to the doctrine of decrees, and insist that while Christ's blood was sufficient for all it is efficacious only for those irresistibly called, the end result is the same. We need only change the wording of the analogy, and say: "What would we think of the shipbuilder who professed concern for the safety of all on board, and provided plenty of lifeboats, then put a skipper in charge who would deliberately allow half the passengers on the sinking ship to *remain asleep in their berths?*"

The burden of these chapters is to declare that the Atonement is designed by God for all, is truly available to all, and that the faith by which justification is experienced is an option to all. There is no public offer to all secretly abridged by God's decrees behind the scenes. There is no dual track of gospel ministration with the Church preaching to all on one track and the Spirit irresistibly calling some and leaving the rest in their sins, on the other track.

Robert Shank effectively dismantles the "paradox" notion. He writes:

> There is nothing about God's gift of believers to be the heritage of the Son who died for them which somehow transforms the Gospel's "whosoever will" into a "whosoever must" and a "most of you shan't." There is nothing about it which binds men in the straitjacket of an antecedent decree of positive unconditional election and reprobation, while insisting that they are "free." There is nothing about it which conjures up

some dark, inscrutable paradox, loudly insisting upon the impossibility of reconciling Holy Scripture's revelation of both the sovereignty of God and the moral freedom and accountability of men. It is only some men's theology which does such things. All theologians to the contrary notwithstanding, the Scriptures declare that, with respect to both the saved and the lost, God takes fully into account the faculty of spiritual initiative and decision with which He endowed man in creation. He has respect for His own creatures.[4]

The Inescapable Clarity of Scripture

The Scriptures abundantly confirm Shank. The declarations of God's will concerning all are too unambiguous for debate. Intercession in prayer "for all men" is pleasing to God "who desires all men to be saved and to come to the knowledge of the truth" (1 Timothy 2:1, 4). And can anyone imagine a God who urges "intercession" for all men when He has secretly determined not to save all men? This would plant in the very command to intercede a stain of insincerity and duplicity. Here would be an intercession doomed to failure not because the sinner rested in full moral responsibility but because God blocked the intercession—the very intercession which He himself had authorized! What kind of God would this be?

According to Peter the Second Coming is deferred because God "is long-suffering...not willing that anyone should perish but that all should come to repentance" (2 Peter 3:9). To repentance, yet withhold saving faith from some? This would be teasing, like a cat playing with a mouse.

How clearly is the universality of the Atonement declared by the apostle John. Christ in His death "is the propitiation for our sins, and not for ours only but also for the whole world" (1 John 2:2). If Christ died for all, then salvation is available to all. If available it is available to all on the same terms—personal faith.

The clear Biblical teaching is that God wills that all should benefit by Christ's death. *This* should be the compass point from which we take all our theological bearings. Having established thus our position we will have no trouble with the few passages which seem to place a limit on God's saving provision.

Anthony A. Hoekema thinks that a limitation is taught in Matthew 1:21, "You shall call His name JESUS, for He will save His people from their sins," with "His people" implying a select group.[5] But such an interpretation flies so directly in the face of the rest of Scripture—such as John's proclamation that Jesus is the "Lamb of God who takes away the sin of the world!" (John 1:29)—that we are compelled to seek an alternative explanation. The New Testament which follows makes it clear that we become "His people" by faith. What the passage teaches is not a limitation in the beneficiaries of Christ's mission, but a declaration of the content, or nature, of the salvation: it will not be from the Romans but *from sin*. And so Paul: "Christ Jesus came into the would to save sinners" (I Timothy 1:15).[6]

The Stages of Faith

Before leaving our inquiry concerning the divine plan for faith's availability, we should point out that faith is often—in fact, quite generally—acquired in stages. The most clear-cut distinction is between the intellectual l staX and the spiritual-reality stage, when belief becomes experience.

The genesis of faith is in the moment of perception of truth. When by the Spirit one is awakened to the reality of Christ, and perceives the staggering fact of the Resurrection, intellectual faith is born. It is impossible to say, "I see that" without in the same breath saying "I believe that." From this moment on the basic elements of Christianity are a datum of consciousness.

This is, however, not yet saving faith. One must choose one's reaction to this discovery. Perception of Christ in the mind, even with full persuasion of truth, may not be followed by surrender and obedience. Believing that this bus is going where I want to go will not get me there if I do not get on. The faith of the mind must become the faith of the feet.

The initial stage of faith is produced by spiritual awakening and revelation. The saving stage is the choice to make this Christ my own, and to believingly accept what He is offering to me Faith is then a mutual giving and receiving, an exchange of intimate, radical commitments, a true person-to-person encounter with Christ. When this occurs faith and assurance are equivalent. The faith of the mind has become the faith of the heart.

Of course the perception/reception stages may be so close as to seem to be simultaneous. Many yield to Christ instantly, without a struggle or time-gap, the moment they perceive Him as Saviour. But because of previous cultural conditioning, persons brought up in the church may find it more difficult to bridge the gap between intellectual belief and saving faith.

This is to say that the embryonic, or intellectual, level of faith may be experienced as a sudden, sometimes unexpected, illumination, a discovery of the Truth as it is in Jesus; or it may be acquired through environment. John Wesley is an example of the latter. The basic doctrines of the Christian faith were so built into his thinking, virtually from infancy, that there never was a time that he consciously disbelieved in Jesus as the Son of God Saviour. This theological anchor motivated him in the days of the Holy Club, his endeavor to win the 'heathen" in Georgia, and in his searchings with the Moravians. But according to his own analysis, during all these years he had the faith of a servant, not a son.[7] It was not until Sunday night, May 24, 1738, that his faith became the trust of assurance—when he could grasp the reality that Christ died for *him*, John Wesley.

What was the problem before? It was not that he lacked the intellectual level of faith concerning Christ's identity and Calvary mission, but that he did not comprehend the simplicity of the "Just as I Am' kind of faith that appropriates the merits of Christ's blood for oneself—*now*. He had been for years a believer, but not a receiver. The roadblock had been an attempt to achieve assurance by works—an attempt of which he up to this time had been only dimly aware.

But even a personal encounter can be destroyed by drawing back from its terms and implications. For the nature of faith does not change in the initial new birth experience. A saving relationship with Christ continues to depend on a vital (not "feigned," 1 Timothy 1:5, KJV) faith, and the constituent elements of this faith are as essential for the faith's very existence ten years after the new birth as they are in the moment of the new birth.

To suppose that the relationship is locked in by virtue of either a "finished salvation' kind of Atonement, or by some divine eternal decree, apart from the moral involvement of a living, ongoing faith, is to empty the relationship of all moral content and personal vitality—which is to say, *reality*.[8]

Endnotes

1. *Saved By Grace*), p. 78. Zane C. Hodges also affirms the inherent conflict in God between His desire to save all and His decree to save some: "But what God *desires* to come to pass, and what in His wisdom He *decrees* will come to pass, are not always the same thing," *Absolutely Free*, (Zondervan, 1989), p. 73.

2. Quoted by Hoekema, *Saved By Grace*, p. 79.

3. Ibid.

4. *Life In the Son* (Springfield, Missouri: Westcott Publishers, 1961), p. 341. Now published by Bethany House Pub., Minneapolis, Minn. Quotation by permission of author.

5. *Saved By Grace*, p. 57.

6. Surely we cannot make sense of "save sinners" unless it means salvation from their sin. A salvation from hell which could not save from the sin which creates hell would be a colossal failure.

7. *Works*, VII, 199, 236.

8. See Shank, pp. 340-344 for a helpful treatment of Romans 9-11. For further treatment of divine sovereignty and supposed election passages see Purkiser, Taylor, Taylor, *God, Man, and Salvation* (Beacon Hill Press of Kansas City, 1977), pp. 424-438; H. Ray Dunning, *Grace, Faith, and Holiness* (Beacon Hill Press of Kansas City, 1988), pp. 435f, 507f; and H. Orton Wiley, *Christian Theology* (Nazarene Publishing House, 1941), 2:334-40.

Chapter Ten
Putty or Person?

WE HAVE STRESSED THE volitional nature of faith, as being what we choose to do. But what about the conversions which seem to come right "out of the blue"? When there seems to be no conscious decision to believe, but a discovery, sometimes completely unexpected, that we do believe, and we are as surprised as anyone? Faith sort of creeps up on us and catches us on our blind side.

Surprise Conversions

Naturally everyone thinks at once of Saul, being confronted by Jesus on the road to Damascus. How could he do other than believe? Even the Philippian jailer, to whom the command was given, "Believe on the Lord Jesus and you will be saved," found himself in an overwhelming set of events which would make unbelief very difficult. After all, if your prize prisoner has been preaching the gospel (you have heard something of it) and now the infinite God comes to his rescue with an earthquake, wouldn't it be quite natural to believe whatever this God-delivered man told you to believe?

The history of the church sparkles with such conversions; and in our day as well as past days. C. S. Lewis tells about his capture by faith in *Surprised by Joy*. The case of Victor Hamilton is especially unique. Somewhere between brushing his teeth, he reports, and the bedroom, he was arrested by the Spirit. In the bedroom he fell on his knees and began to pray. His older brother looked at him in astonishment and said, "What's up?" Victor replied: "I think I've just been converted." And indeed he was, as every subsequent day has demonstrated.

Do these experiences confirm the understanding of faith as a divinely infused gift, i.e., the action of God in regeneration upon passive recipients? If so, then the discovery of the truth, its inward saving effects, and our awareness of faith are simultaneous, all constituting one divine moment in the irresistible action of the Spirit.

But not so fast. In each case there was a profound degree of hunger and a deep searching, even beneath the external bluff of skepticism. When confronted with the truth there was a glad willingness to believe. The set of the soul was already reaching for God, rather than hostile. Saul (who became Paul) was not a rebel against God, but passionately jealous for the purity of his God-ordained Jewish faith. It was in honesty that he was furiously marching to Damascus that day; a special revelation was thoroughly warranted. And Victor Hamilton was deeply aware of the constant prayers of his father and many others for him. Inward pressure toward God had been building up, even though he might not have been fully aware of what was happening.

Conversion Always an Option

While some conversions seem to be irresistible, God is never in the business of chloroforming the will to achieve His ends.[1] We are compelled to affirm that at every point free moral agency remains intact and unbattered.

While C. S. Lewis speaks of his conversion as being "dragged through the doorway,"[2] he does not really intend for us to understand him to mean that his will was overpowered. Elsewhere he reminds us that Jesus urged people to "count the cost" before becoming Christians. He has Jesus saying, that even after conversion, "You have free will, and if you choose, you can push Me away."[3]

The ability to push Jesus away either before conversion or afterward is unmistakably confirmed in the Scripture. There are certain graphic sayings of Jesus which are completely irreconcilable with total *monergism* (that hidden in our psyche and circumstances all the strings of motivation are being manipulated by God, on the basis of a predetermined selection).

In considering such issues Jesus' extended discussion in John 3 always draws like a magnet. Certain firm implications taken together create inescapable conclusions. "He who believes in Him," Jesus said of himself, "is not condemned; but he who has not believed is condemned already, because he has not believed in the name of the only begotten Son of God" (v. 18). His condemnation, originally due to his sin, continues to stand because he has refused to turn from sin to Christ in faith. The present participle *me pisteuon,* "is not believing," turns to the perfect indicative, *me pepisteuken,* "has not believed," indicating a refusal to believe. Of this perfect tense A. T. Robertson says: "has taken a permanent attitude of refusal."[4]

This is supported by what immediately follows: "...men loved darkness" (v. 19). It is their love of darkness which prompts unbelief, not inability to believe. The tie-up is at the end of the chapter: "He who believes in the Son has everlasting life; and he who does not believe the Son shall not see life, but the wrath of God abides on him" (v. 36). Rejection is deliberate, willful, and fully accountable. It is what a free agent chooses to do.[5]

Later on Jesus said to the Jews, "You search the Scriptures, for in them you think you have eternal life: and these are they which testify of Me. But you are not willing to come to Me that you may have life" (John 5:39-40). The very sorts of things which happened in the lives of Lewis and Hamilton had been happening all around these Jews, but they had steeled themselves against the obvious. "You are not willing to come"— what an indictment! Not, "You cannot," but "you will not." This implies, furthermore, that Jesus is saying, "If you would, you could." Here is total, unmitigated personal responsibility. To try to sneak in between the lines some notion of secret deprivation of inclination because not given it by God, is to play fast and loose with words, and betray a theological desperation willing to impugn Christ and His Father with insincerity and falseness.

The power of the human will, quite able to defy God even in His sovereignty, is nowhere more poignantly declared than in Jesus' heartbroken cry over Jerusalem: "How often I wanted to gather your children together, as a hen gathers her brood under her wings, but you were not willing!" (Luke 13:34). Not *unable* but *unwilling.* Later Jesus, in a similar dirge, weeps over the city Luke 19:41). In both passages Jesus is declaring His own desire for the city but confesses that His will for the city is blocked completely by its resistance.

If behind the scenes God is pulling the strings, and their "would not" was really "could not," then either Christ was dishonest and the tears were false, or else Christ felt one way and the Father felt another. This would imply a divergence between the Father and Son which would support the little girl who said she liked Jesus but hated God—because Jesus wanted to save people and God wanted to damn them. If all this sounds blasphemous, we can only insist that the real blasphemy is in the doctrine of predestination and effectual calling which can create a schism between what God has decreed to do and what Jesus with tears wants to do. Jesus wanted to save Jerusalem; God withheld the ability to repent. How is that for a "kingdom divided against itself"!

However, a statement in Luke disproves any such rupture in the Trinity. Speaking of the Pharisees and experts in the law, who spurned John's baptism, the inspired writer says: They "rejected the will of God for themselves" (Luke 7:30). God's purpose for them and Christ's purpose were the same. In perfect divine unity the Father and Son had only their redemption in mind. But in the awesome power of free will that redemption was rejected.

It would be difficult to imagine any more graphic or decisive affirmation of the final power of the individual to control his own destiny than the telltale reference to the wedding garment in Jesus' parable of the wedding feast. The broad import of the parable is unmistakable. The wedding feast of Christ and the Church is prophetically in the background of Christ's thought. The primary invitation to the elite was spurned, but the ragamuffins of the highways and byways responded, until the hall was filled with happy guests.

Suddenly a pall drops over the room, when the king notices a man not properly dressed. The significance of this terrible moment will be missed unless we understand that wedding garments were provided by the household where the wedding took place. This man had access to one as well as anyone else. Either he took it and chucked it into a corner, deciding not to wear it; or else he sneaked in a side door thinking he could avoid the wedding garment requirement. But in any case his arrogance didn't work, and he was thrown out—"into the darkness; there will be weeping and gnashing of teeth" (Matthew 22:13; cf. Revelation 19:7-8).

These last words in the parable prove beyond reasonable doubt that Jesus was thinking in eternal terms. This wedding garment symbolized a personal experience of salvation. But the man was without his not because it had been withheld but because he chose not to wear it. This is why when accosted he was "speechless." He had no excuse. Otherwise he could have said, "Sorry, I didn't know such a garment was required," or, "I was not offered one." But he knew he had no excuse—and we are to know equally that we have no excuse.

We dare not even hint that the king (in our case the King) rigged arrangements secretly to keep the man from getting his hands on a wedding garment. Again we must declare that any doctrine which would imply such a maneuver on the part of our King is an inexcusable tampering with Scripture. The truth is obvious and the conclusion is painfully inescapable: He must have the wedding garment. The wedding garment is available. But wearing it is an option with us. Hence, "many are called, but few are chosen" (v. 14). Fewer are chosen than invited because of the stubborn impenitence of some of the invited.[6]

Endnotes

1. That is, His salvation ends. He often controls the wills of men for immediate strategic objectives, as when he moved upon King Artaxerxes to send Nehemiah to Jerusalem. But He stops short of imposing on us the ultimate choice of eternal destiny.

2. The *Joyful Christian* (New York: Collier Books, 1977), p. 32.

3. Ibid., p. 77.

4. *Word Pictures in the New Testament*, Vol. V, p. 52.

5. NASB says "he who does not obey the Son shall not see life."

6. A. B. Bruce says that "the wedding-robe represents Christian holiness, and the demand is that all believers in the gospel shall sedulously cultivate it, "*The Parabolic Teaching of Christ,*, p. 479.

Chapter Eleven
What Abraham Learned

LET US REJOICE IN our freedom! But let us use it wisely, not abuse it. We use it when we choose to cooperate with God every step of the way, from awakening to the Pearly City. There is infinitely more value in our voluntary steps of obedience, than any amount of manipulated steps in passive conformity.

The Psychological Theory of Freedom

Some attempt to follow Jonathan Edwards in his psychological theory of freedom and thereby affirm both freedom and determinism. This theory says that trust and obedience are human responses, and the one trusting and obeying is doing both freely, as far as his own consciousness is concerned. But according to *ultimate determinism* he is only carrying out the compulsions of antecedent motives. He thinks he is choosing in such a way that he could equally have chosen the opposite. In fact he is choosing in the way that the psychological input into his total life and character has predestined him to choose. And the motivational settings have been arranged by God according to His own predetermined plan. So the end result is the same. The trusting and obeying are the response of a pawn being acted upon. It is, in effect, a programmed response, like a programmed missile.[1]

Hence the trusting and obeying have only little if any moral value; that is, they are not truly accountable actions. What is not ultimately accountable to the person as a free agent is neither blameworthy nor praiseworthy. Result: Neither *personal* holiness nor sinfulness is to such a being a moral possibility.

All that is possible is the *amoral* (ethically neutral) holiness of *position*: the sanctity of being owned by God. Such holiness is real in its place, but is as morally neutral as was the holiness of the soil where Moses was standing, when God said, "Take your sandals off your feet, for the place where you stand is holy ground" (Exodus 3:5). Even pawns can be holy in this sense. But this is not good enough for persons. Psychological freedom only is at bottom a mirage.

Post-Conversion Free Agency

At this point (to pick up the theme of the previous chapter), we need to confront squarely the fact that some who have experienced a dramatic conversion later fall away, as the seed that sprang up joyously soon withered because it had no deep root (Luke 8:13). And at any point after conversion, no matter how supernaturally it happened, the believer, especially in times of crisis—of sorrow, temptation, disappointment— can turn away from God, and make shipwreck of his or her faith (I Timothy 1:19). I asked Victor Hamilton: "Have you been aware since your conversion of times when you were tempted to go back on the Lord, and fully aware that you had it in your power to do so?" His answer: "Yes, several times."

The protest that apostasy only proves a defective conversion is so contrary to the facts that it would never be made if there were not an *a priori* theory to defend. But as usual here too our arbiter is the Scripture. One of the best ways to unfold this is to see how consistently the Scripture assumes that saving faith must be persevering. While in one sense Jesus is "the author and finisher of our faith," the command to "run with endurance the race that is set before us" is given to *us*, not to Jesus (Hebrews 12:1-2)

When God promised Abraham a son, and assured him that his descendants would be as uncountable as the stars in the heavens, Abraham believed God, and the record says that God "reckoned it to him as righteousness" (Genesis 15:6, NASB). Paul seizes upon this in his argument that in Christ we are justified by faith rather than by works. In Romans 4 he quotes the statement three times (vv. 3, 9, 22; cf. Galatians 3:6) with a very simple application: not only did the verse explain the nature of Abraham's righteousness but it explains the nature of ours. "Now not for his sake only was it written, that it was reckoned to him, but for our sake also, to whom it [righteousness] will be reckoned as those who believe in Him who raised Jesus...who was delivered up because of our transgressions, and was raised because of our justification" (vv. 23-24, NASB).

God accounts our faith as righteousness. This is to say, He accounts us as righteous (justified in His sight) on the simple basis of believing—in *Abraham's* case, of believing God's *promise;* in our case, of believing the justifying power of what God *has done in Christ.*

Now the fact that James quotes the same Genesis statement as proof that Abraham was justified "by works" is profoundly significant, and dare not be missed. The time between the initial accrediting of Abraham's faith as righteousness (Genesis 15:6) and his obedience in offering Isaac was some 27 years. But James takes the pronouncement of Genesis 15:6 and applies it to Abraham's demonstration of faith on Mt. Moriah. In this act of obedience, he says, "the Scripture was fulfilled which says, 'And Abraham believed God, and it was reckoned to him for righteousness'" (James 2:21-23, NASB). The *kind of faith* which back there was imputed as righteousness finds its *definition* on Mt. Moriah.

From James we learn two things about justifying faith. First, justifying faith continues to justify only as long as it remains valid faith, rather than empty presumption. Abraham was not locked into a justified relationship to God by one single act of faith. Rather faith had to be maintained as continuous trust and confidence.

Second, true justifying faith is obedient. It was through obedience that Abraham's faith "was perfected" (James 2:22, NASB). And James' whole argument is that this is equally true with us. The *obedience of faith* is not the kind of "works" Paul was repudiating. It is rather the kind of work which belongs to the very nature of justifying faith, and without which it cannot exist.

John MacArthur believes in the persevering and obedience nature of faith but still affirms non-forfeitable eternal security. This can only be done by postulating a kind of irresistible grace which assures the *maintenance* of trust and obedience. This means that whatever freedom the person might have had before conversion is now swallowed up in divine manipulation and management.

This—it needs to be repeated—is reduction from personhood to pawnhood. A pawn is any piece on the chessboard of life which has no real option in its moves. The chess player moves it—*period.*

But a doctrine of salvation which sees the pieces as persons rather than as pawns, sees faith as a free choice all along the board. While the faith is aided by the Spirit, it is not infused one-sidedly, neither is it preserved one-sidedly, with God being the only real actor. The believer is not only a free person in choosing to believe initially, but he is free in his believing (and obeying, which is implied by "believing") every moment thereafter. He is as capable of returning to unbelief from faith ten or twenty years down the line as he was capable of turning from unbelief to faith at the beginning. Every warning, every exhortation in the Bible assumes this. This understanding prompted Barnabas to encourage the new converts in Antioch "that with purpose of heart they should continue with the Lord" Acts 11:28).

Dale Yocum pins the matter down admirably:

> The high Calvinists were at least consistent when they asserted that the reprobate are not free to receive Christ, and the elect are not free to reject Him. The modern "eternal security people" have abandoned that consistency when they declare that sinners are free to receive Christ (through the aid of the Spirit), but once having believed they are no longer free to reject Him (through resisting the Spirit). To imply that saving grace deprives individuals of one of the fundamental attributes of their humanity, their moral freedom, is entirely unreasonable and unsupported by Scripture.[2]

It is understandable that many timid souls shrink from facing up to their personal responsibility in being true to Christ. They exclaim, "This teaching robs me of my feeling of security." "How do I know that I won't backslide some time down in the future, and lose my salvation?"

To such persons we must say, "Sorry, but that is totally up to you. Plenty of grace is available for you to cling to the Lord if you want to avail yourself of it. If you choose not to, no one is to blame but yourself. You cannot 'pass the buck' to anyone else, even to Jesus."

Whether we like it or not, we must accept the responsibility of our freedom. We cannot evade it by hiding behind a doctrine which teaches us to shift all responsibility to God.

The "feeling" of security that "eternal security" people have is the delusion of a false security, and the sooner the spell of this delusion is broken the better. Only those who at this moment are "in Christ" are secure this moment. And only those who obey Christ tomorrow will be secure tomorrow—and the next day, and all the days after that. As one church leader said, bearing such a responsibility "keeps us on our toes."

And it wraps around us the solid comfort of a *true* security. "For I am persuaded," exults Paul, "that neither death nor life, nor angels nor principalities nor powers, or things present nor things to come, nor height nor depth, nor any other created thing, shall be able to separate us from the love of God which is in Christ Jesus our Lord" (Romans 8:38-39).[3]

Endnotes

1. Compare the psychological determinism of B. F. Skinner and of behaviorism generally. Conscience is simply a conditioned reflex.

2. *Creeds In Contrast: A Study in Calvinism and Arminianism* (Salem, Ohio: Schmul Publishing Co., Inc., 1986), p. 137.

3. This is often quoted as "proof" of unconditional security, but Paul has already warned us earlier in the chapter that "if we live according to the flesh" we will die (v. 13), and that we are "heirs of God and joint heirs with Christ, if indeed we suffer with him' (v. 17). Nothing outside ourselves can separate us from Christ, and Christ will never separate Himself from us. But we can choose to step outside that sphere of security and go back to the ways of the flesh and refuse to "suffer" with Christ, if we choose. The promise of true security is to those who "love God" (v. 28).

Chapter Twelve
Where Do We Now Stand?

WHAT BEARING THEN DOES a Biblical understanding of saving faith have on our doctrine of the Atonement? We are compelled to conclude that a doctrine which teaches a finished salvation in the sense of non-forfeitable accomplishment, cannot be true. For the Bible links the efficacy of the Atonement to personal faith, and also teaches a faith which is voluntary and individual; aided by the Holy Spirit but not irresistibly caused.

Faith is seen in the Scriptures as an option which is genuine, not fictional. This means that the Atonement can be said to be objective and finished only in the sense that full provision has been made, and full propitiation accomplished, making possible the salvation of all who will believe. The fullness of the provision at Calvary becomes transmuted at the personal level into real salvation when and if the individual appropriates the merit of the blood by faith.

As A. W. Tozer writes: *"Before redemption becomes effective toward the individual man there is an act which that man must do. That act is not one of merit, but of condition"* (italics his).[1] It is the act of believing out of a desperately repentant heart.

If Christ's death accomplished a "finished salvation" in the sense that it assured unconditionally the eternal salvation of all *for whom He died*, then we are caught on the horns of a dilemma. If He died *for all*, then all will be saved. Every human being ever born into the human race will ultimately be in heaven, no matter what he does or does not do. But if the Bible plainly teaches that all will not be saved, then the conclusion is that Christ died only for the elect—hence we have what is called a Limited Atonement.

We escape the dilemma only if we recognize what the Bible clearly teaches, that Christ's death was *for* all but *provisional*. This is, salvation is provided for all and offered to all, but on clearly specified moral terms.

Provisional thus means conditional, and the condition is the faith which turns from sin in true penitence, turns to God in true surrender and trust, and rests solely in the mercy of God and the merits of the blood.

A secretly infused faith, irresistible and selective, would imply a limited atonement, or else completely refute any notion of a "finished transaction." If the Atonement is sufficient for all (as some Calvinists hold) yet not efficacious for all, then the Atonement cannot be in its very nature a transaction between the Father and the Son which *accomplishes* the salvation of *any*.

A selectively infused faith would make a mockery of moral responsibility. In addition, it would be a testimony to the colossal failure of divine grace. Grace which is imposed is not grace but force. Only the influence which woos and enables can bear the sacred name of grace.

Moreover, the Atonement does not provide a permanent "fix" for the sins of the believer, past, present, and future. This would be an immoral system, unworthy of a holy God. It indeed would be the scandal of pre-forgiveness.

There is never a time, whether before conversion or afterwards, that we dare approach the Father in any other way than that prescribed by John: "If we confess our sins, he is faithful and just to forgive us our sins and to cleanse us from all unrighteousness" (1 John 1:9).

It is not evangelical faith which presumes to claim the merit of Christ's atoning death while ignoring this "If." It is rather pretentious and delusive presumption. The faith that confesses—with all that Biblical confession implies—can rest comfortably in the assurance that Christ's blood has enabled a holy Father-God to be both "faithful and just" in forgiving us. God's love prompts His faithfulness, while the Blood enables Him to forgive in justice.

Endnotes
1. *Paths to Power* (Camp Hill, PA: Christian Publications, Inc., 1966), p. 16.

For Further Reading

Hartley, John F. and R. Larry Shelton, editors, *An Inquiry Into Soteriology from a Biblical Theological Perspective* Anderson, IN: Warner Press, Inc., 1981), primarily pp. 195-263.

Purkiser, W. T., Richard S. Taylor, Willar H. Taylor, *God, Man & Salvation A Biblical Theology* (Kansas City, MO: Beacon Hill Press of Kansas City, 1977), pp. 410-438.

Purkiser, W. T., *Security: The False and the True* (Kansas City, MO: Beacon Hill Press of Kansas City, 1956)

Rice, Richard, *God's Foreknowledge & Man's Free Will* (Minneapolis: Bethany House Publishers, 1985).

Shank, Robert, *Life in the Son: A Study in the Doctrine of Perseverance* (Springfield, MO: Westcott Publishers, 1961).

Taylor, Richard S., *A Right Conception of Sin* (Kansas City, MO: Nazarene Publishing House, 1939.

Wood, Laurence W., *Truly Ourselves, Truly the Spirit's* (Grand Rapids, MI: Francis Asbury Press of Zondervan, 1989).

Yocum, Dale M., *Creeds in Contrast* (Salem, OH: Schmul Publishing Co., Inc. 1986).